In this entirely updated edition of their classic *Namibia*, first published in 1999 and having sold over 40 000 copies in various languages and editions, master photographers Gerald and Marc Hoberman have returned to Namibia to capture the essence of this awe-inspiring country and celebrate its many unique facets through more than 450 large-scale, full-colour photographs, accompanied by fascinating and entertaining text. From land and air, the renowned South African father-and-son team have covered the length and breadth of this immense country – from the arid Karas region of the south to the north-eastern wetlands of the Caprivi, from the treacherous Skeleton Coast shores to the colossal sand dunes of Sossusvlei and beyond. Namibia's rich cultural diversity is represented here too, from the ancient cultures of the San, Himba and Herero, to the colonial-inspired seaside towns of Lüderitz and Swakopmund and the bustling modern African city of Windhoek. And then there's the abundant wildlife, the luxurious lodges, the unexplained mysteries and the surprising moments of serendipity, so essential for an African adventure – these are the elements that make up the extraordinary tapestry of this extraordinary land.

NAMIBIA

GERALD & MARC HOBERMAN

NAMIBIA

GERALD & MARC HOBERMAN

photography by

GERALD & MARC HOBERMAN

with text by

MARC HOBERMAN

and a foreword by

HIS EXCELLENCY
HIFIKEPUNYE POHAMBA
PRESIDENT OF THE REPUBLIC OF NAMIBIA

HOBERMAN
PHOTOGRAPHIC PUBLISHERS
CAPE TOWN · LONDON · NAMIBIA

Concept, Photography, Design and Production Control: Gerald Hoberman, Marc Hoberman
Colour Reproduction: Marc Hoberman
Text: Marc Hoberman
Copy Editing: Joy Clack
Layout: Marc Hoberman, Melanie Kriel
Cartographer: Peter Slingsby
Indexing: Joy Clack

www.hobermancollection.com

ISBN: 978-99916-792-7-3

Namibia is published by The Gerald & Marc Hoberman Collection (Pty) Ltd
Reg. No. 99/00167/07. Unit 10, Frazzitta Business Park, Freedom Way, Milnerton 7441, Cape Town, South Africa
Telephone: +27 (0)21 551 0270 Fax: +27 (0)21 555 1935
e-mail: sales@hobermancollection.com

International marketing, corporate sales and picture library

United Kingdom, Republic of Ireland, Europe
Hoberman Collection UK
Aston House, Cornwall Avenue, London N3 1LF
Telephone: +44 (0)208 371 3021
e-mail: sales@hobermancollection.com

United States of America, Canada, Asia
Hoberman Collection USA, Inc. / Una Press, Inc.
601 N Congress Ave. Ste. 201, Delray Beach FL 33445
Telephone: +1 561 542 1141
e-mail: hobermanusa@gmail.com

Books may be purchased in bulk at discounted prices for corporate and promotional gifts. We also offer special editions, personalised covers, dust jackets and corporate imprints, including tip-in pages and gold foiling, tailored to meet your needs.

Agents and distributors

South Africa	*Namibia*	*United Kingdom*	*United States of America & Canada*
10 Frazzitta Business Park	Projects & Promotions cc	DJ Segrue Ltd	Perseus Distribution
Freedom Way, Milnerton	PO Box 656	7c Bourne Road	387 Park Avenue South
Cape Town, South Africa	Omaruru	Bushey, Hertfordshire	New York
Tel: +27 (0)21 551 0270	Tel: +264 (0)64 571 376	WD23 3NH	NY 10016
Fax: +27 (0)21 555 1935	Fax: +264 (0)64 571 379	Tel: +44 (0)208 421 9521	Tel: +1 800 343 4499
e-mail: office@hobermancollection.com	e-mail: proprom@iafrica.com.na	Fax: +44 (0)208 421 9577	e-mail: hobermanusa@gmail.com
		e-mail: sales@djsegrue.co.uk	

Printed in China

ACKNOWLEDGEMENTS

Producing a book of this scale, especially about a land of such magnitude, is no mean feat and could never have been put together without the exceptional help of many exceptional people. Namibia, we discovered, is not short of such people, passionate about their country, enthusiastic to help and eager to share knowledge.

Firstly, with respect and gratitude, we would like to thank His Excellency Hifikepunye Pohamba for his immeasurable support of this project and providing us with the book's foreword. We also extend our appreciation to Permanent Secretary Samuel Hendrik /Gôagoseb for his enthusiasm and insight, as well as the staff at State House, in particular Penny Muyunda and Fillemon Nangonya.

Thank you to the HOBERMAN team 'holding the fort' back home – Magda Bosch, Jacqueline van Zyl, Marine Lindeque, Graham Richardson, Gavin Smith and Melissa Schrikker, and our designer-extraordinaire (who just so happens to be from Tsumeb), Melanie Kriel.

Thank you to all of the lodges that hosted us and restaurants that fed us, we've become forever rich with friends and memories.

A small paragraph in an acknowledgements section will never do justice to thanking Monica Spall, but we'll have a go! Friend, business partner, confidante, comrade and inspiring whirlwind of energy and passion, Monica has worked with the two of us for well over a decade and still impressively has the energy and patience to carry on. Monica is the owner of Projects & Promotions, the exclusive agent for HOBERMAN products, and the driving force behind the success of HOBERMAN in Namibia. We take this opportunity to thank you for your invaluable support and friendship over the years and look forward to many years to come.

Below is a list of people to whom we give extra special thanks. There have been so many along our journey, unfortunately too many to list and undoubtedly we've left someone out – if that's you, you'll know who you are and the next round will be on us!

GERALD & MARC HOBERMAN

Aaron Xoagub
André Etsebeth
André Louw
Anja Schröder
Bonifatius Nehale
Brett Southworth, Leon Kotze
Carol-Jean Rechter
Charles LoBello, Christina Holbrook, Joe Shum
   (Qualibre)
Chris Muth
Christine 'Luki' Boois
Daan Herman
Dale Pepler, George Hopking
Danie Holloway
Frik Orban
Guy Nockels, Elnette Pearson, Gwen Swart
Hanne Marott-Alpers
Jaco Klynsmith, Elmarie Janse van Rensburg
   (Trustco)

Jan Arnold (Bidvest)
Joe Gross
Joyce Moggridge
Juan Claassen
Kate Echement, Matthew Cleverley
   (N/a'an ku sê Foundation)
Kathrin Schaefer-Stiege, Noag Kairua, Kira
   Rohloff, Claudia Franke, Elli Gamke, Sahra
   Rosana (Okakambe Trails riders)
Keiko Matsuda (NHK Media)
Kelly Hicks, Bobby Jo Bassingthwaighte
Madri Frewer (First National Bank)
Manni Goldbeck
Dr Margaret Jacobsohn
Megan Wise
Monica Toibo
Moose McGregor
Noah and Liam Spall
Olga Kausch

Paul Joubert
Paulus P. Nelongo
Penda Shimali
Pieter Grobler
Quinten Potgieter, Sanja van den Berg
   (Old Mutual)
Raymond Spall
Rita Lok
Robert and Birgit Momsen (Scenic Air)
Stella Auala (De Beers Marine)
Tanya de Bruyne
Thomas and Reeze Becker
Tommy and Kit Collard
Zak the Dog

INTRODUCTION

by Gerald & Marc Hoberman

Twenty seven thousand seven hundred and thirty three kilometres, open-plain horseback riding, fixed-wing planes, helicopters, microlights, quad bikes, hot-air balloons, dug-out canoes, speed boats, river boats, juggernauts, ox-carts, a Land Rover Defender (named Olive), a VW Caddy, Suzuki Jimny, Toyota Condor, six wheel changes and three bottles of Jägermeister – Namibia is nothing short of an adventure!

The production of this book took place over three life-changing years, in which we covered the length and breadth of the country, and gave us the opportunity to rediscover what made us fall in love with Namibia in the first place – not that we ever really forgot, but it's always a treat to do it all over again!

In 1999 we set out on one of our many father-and-son photographic expeditions. The destination was Namibia, a country we had read about countless times and seen endless inspiring images of, yet we had never before experienced first-hand. Driving from our hometown of Cape Town we crossed the South Africa/Namibia border at Noordoewer and were met with the sheer majesty of Namibia's ancient, arid south – a theatre of geological wonders, silent, vast and pristine. The Namibia 'bug' had bit and we travelled, cameras-a-clicking, through the immense country to its most northern parts of Ohangwena and the lush Caprivi, marvelling all the way at the staggering diversity packed into one country.

A land of extremes, here one finds the world's highest sand dunes, plants some 2 000 years old, a canyon rivalled in size only by Colorado's Grand Canyon, and two spectacular distinctive deserts – the Kalahari and the Namib (the latter considered our planet's oldest desert). Here one also finds the biggest population of free-roaming cheetah and the world's largest underground lake, as well as the largest open-cast uranium mine. Namibia played host to the largest meteorite shower ever discovered and its Hoba meteorite, weighing more than 50 tonnes, is some 80 000 years old. Wherever one travels, the people of Namibia are friendly, proud, united, and steeped in tradition. The country's cultures are as varied and rich as its landscapes: from the ancient San, Namibia's earliest inhabitants renowned for their rock art (some examples dating back 28 000 years), 'click' language and astonishing knowledge of the land, to the statuesque ochre-covered Himba and the head-to-toe curiously and colourfully-attired Herero. The proud Ovambo people, steeped in historical significance, make up approximately half of the country's population, and remain strongly active in the country's governance. These are but a few of the many peoples and cultures found throughout the country, which is almost incongruously the second least densely populated country on earth. The remnants of Namibia's German colonial past is still evident throughout the country, the German language remains ever popular, while some of the best-preserved colonial buildings on the African continent line the streets of Swakopmund.

Independence finally came to Namibia in 1990 with Sam Nujoma sworn in as the first President of Namibia, to an audience of representatives from 147 countries, including twenty heads of state, as well as Nelson Mandela, who had been released from prison shortly beforehand. Some fifteen years later, in 2005, Dr Nujoma was succeeded by current President, His Excellency Hifikepunye Pohamba, and Namibia remains renowned for its excellent governance and stable political climate. As testament to this, in 2013, global business and financial news provider Bloomberg named Namibia the top emerging market economy in Africa. The Constitution of Namibia is the first constitution to include a provision for environmental protection and approximately 13.6 per cent of the country's surface area is protected, either as a nature reserve, recreation area or game park.

Our special father-and-son journey resulted in our first of many collaborative coffee-table books – *Namibia by Gerald & Marc Hoberman* – which was launched in Windhoek's Tintenpalast later that year, receiving a citation from the then President Sam Nujoma. Over the following years *Namibia* was translated into four languages, released in four different book formats and sold over 40 000 copies internationally. Although our subsequent book projects have taken us far and wide, whenever asked the inevitable question 'so where is the best place you've been?' we're both at first rather non-committal (for correctness-sake) and if (very slightly) hard-pressed the answer's always the same 'Namibia!'

In 2010, we could no longer resist but to update our original book, and somewhere amidst all the fun we've ended up with an entirely new edition instead of an update! Still, the photographers are the same, the author's the same and so is the passion, so we've given the book the same name and let's just all pretend that this is simply the 'revised' edition.

Our hope for this book is that it will inspire you to explore this vast and powerful land, whether you are planning a visit, lucky enough to be a local or have done some exploring already… in Namibia there is always something more to discover.

GERALD & MARC HOBERMAN

NAMIBIA

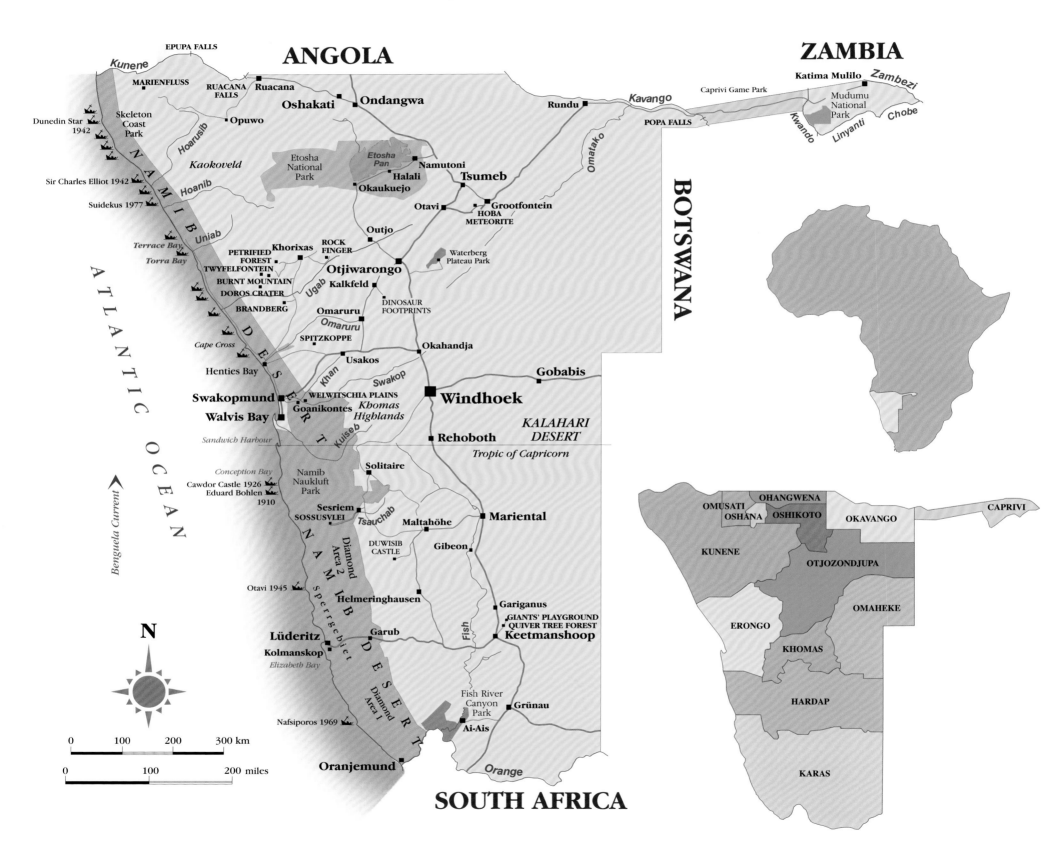

ZAMBIA

ANGOLA

BOTSWANA

SOUTH AFRICA

ATLANTIC OCEAN

Benguela Current

EPUPA FALLS
Kunene
MARIENFLUSS
RUACANA FALLS
Ruacana
Oshakati
Ondangwa
Rundu
Kavango
Caprivi Game Park
Katima Mulilo
Zambezi
Mudumu National Park
Chobe
Linyanti
Kwando
POPA FALLS

Dunedin Star 1942
Skeleton Coast Park
Opuwo
Hoarusib
Kaokoveld
Etosha National Park
Etosha Pan
Namutoni
Halali
Okaukuejo
Tsumeb
Omatako

Sir Charles Elliot 1942
Hoanib
Suidekus 1977
Otavi
Grootfontein
HOBA METEORITE

Terrace Bay
Uniab
Outjo
Waterberg Plateau Park

Torra Bay
PETRIFIED FOREST
Khorixas
ROCK FINGER
TWYFELFONTEIN
Otjiwarongo
BURNT MOUNTAIN
Kalkfeld
DOROS CRATER
Ugab
BRANDBERG
DINOSAUR FOOTPRINTS
Omaruru
Omaruru
Cape Cross
SPITZKOPPE
Okahandja
Usakos
Swakop
Gobabis
Henties Bay
Khan
WELWITSCHIA PLAINS
Swakopmund
Goanikontes
Khomas Highlands
Windhoek
Walvis Bay
Sandwich Harbour
Kuiseb
Rehoboth
KALAHARI DESERT
Tropic of Capricorn
Conception Bay
Cawdor Castle 1926
Eduard Bohlen 1910
Namib Naukluft Park
Solitaire
Sesriem
SOSSUSVLEI
Tsauchab
Maltahöhe
Mariental
Diamond Area 2
DUWISIB CASTLE
Gibeon
Otavi 1945
Helmeringhausen
Gariganus
GIANTS' PLAYGROUND
Sperrgebiet
QUIVER TREE FOREST
Lüderitz
Garub
Keetmanshoop
Kolmanskop
Fish
Elizabeth Bay
NAMIB DESERT
Fish River Canyon Park
Grünau
Nafsiporos 1969
Ai-Ais
Diamond Area 1
Oranjemund
Orange

N

0   100   200   300 km

0   100   200 miles

OMUSATI
OHANGWENA
OSHANA
OSHIKOTO
OKAVANGO
CAPRIVI
KUNENE
OTJOZONDJUPA
OMAHEKE
ERONGO
KHOMAS
HARDAP
KARAS

FOREWORD

Namibia offers a diversity of culture and heritage. It is a peaceful country blessed with a rich and ancient tapestry of people and cultures, differed in their history, languages and beliefs, yet with a palpable sense of pride, all mightily united as Namibians.

It is an extraordinary vast land covering 824 269 square kilometres and encompassing an endless array of stunning contrasts sculpted by the elements over millions of years. Namibia is home to the world's oldest and perhaps most beautiful desert, overflowing with geological wonders, bountiful wildlife, abundant flora and imposing dunes. Its sheer power is matched only by the immense Atlantic Ocean, whose icy Benguela Current meets with a sandy sea of dunes along Namibia's magnificent coastline, bringing not only a wealth of marine life but also vital life-sustaining moisture to the desert from the coast.

Throughout Namibia's distinct regions, landscapes playfully change: the highlands of the central plateau are characterised by deep valleys, rugged hills and massive mountains – some rising nearly 2 000 metres, while the lush north-eastern region of the Caprivi is blessed with an abundance of water from flowing rivers and fertile floodplains.

From fauna to flora, terrain to culture, Namibia's inherent treasures are never taken for granted and a strong culture of protection, conservation and education remains unfailingly high on Namibia's agenda. Namibia is proud to be the first African country to incorporate protection of the environment in its National Constitution. The creation of communal conservancies has given people living in communal areas the opportunity to manage and benefit from their natural resources, together with government and NGOs. Populations of precious wildlife continue to be successfully protected, including black rhino, lions and cheetahs. Namibia has also made history as the first country to designate its entire coastline a national park.

Namibia's secure and sturdy economy continues to grow apace with exciting developments, particularly in the agriculture, fishing, mining and tourism sectors, and the Namibian Government has pursued free-market economic principles designed to promote commercial development and job creation to bring disadvantaged Namibians into the economic mainstream.

Namibia has also joined the international trend towards a 'green economy', with strong actively-pursued goals in sustainable development. Internationally, Namibia is recognised as a biodiversity success story. Indeed, there has never been a better time to invest in Namibia and become part of the African continent's most dynamic economies.

Namibia is a land so bold, so vast and so remarkable that there is no true substitute to behold its breathtaking existence other than by first-hand experience. Those who live in Namibia and those who have visited will understand the almost primeval feeling that can arise from being part of a Namibian landscape. Yet Namibia is also a visual feast and dream for the photographer, presenting endless and myriad opportunities to inspire the eye and heart.

While commending the photographers for their extraordinary work, I invite you to discover or, re-discover our beautiful country Namibia through the pages of this remarkable book.

His Excellency Hifikepunye Pohamba
PRESIDENT OF THE REPUBLIC OF NAMIBIA

FISH RIVER & THE DEEP SOUTH

A geological wonderland of silent, vast, powerful landscapes

Namibia's 'deep south', as it is often referred to, is a vast, arid theatre of geological wonders. Its immense landscapes of gravel plains, craggy mountains, dry savannah and rolling red dunes stretches from the desolate Namib in the west to the Kalahari in the east. This is pristine nature at its best.

Peaceful, tranquil, ancient, Namibia's southern region is filled with fascinating geological phenomena, the awe-inspiring scale of which is perhaps unrivalled in the world. Undoubtedly the best known and most visited of these is the mighty Fish River Canyon. Carved into its present shape over millions of years, this ancient geological spectacle is 161 kilometres long and 27 kilometres wide, with an imposing depth of 550 metres, making it the second largest canyon in the world, comparable only to America's Grand Canyon.

Moments from the Karas Region settlement of Asab, the Mukurob stood sentinel for thousands of years and was one of the country's most visited sites. Also known as The Finger of God or Vingerklip (Afrikaans for 'finger rock'), this fascinating and distinctive geological feature stood 12 metres high and up to 4.5 metres wide, weighing some 450 tonnes. But what made the Mukurob unique was its base – just 3 metres long and 1.5 metres wide, it was narrower than the mass of rock that it supported, which resulted in a curious and bold 'balancing act' of nature. Once part of the Weissrand Plateau, 50 000 years of erosion slowly isolated the structure from the rest of the plateau, creating its unusual shape and inspiring local Nama tales and legends over many generations, as well as firing the imaginations of visitors from all over the world. In the early hours of 8 December 1988, the 34-metre (111.5-foot)-high pinnacle toppled over due to the inevitable gradual weakening of its narrow mudstone neck, and possibly aided by the Spitak earthquake in Armenia, which registered strongly on the seismograph in Windhoek on the previous night. Still standing is its National Monument status.

Namibia's southern region, with its harsh climate and topography, is sparsely populated with great distances between small settlements and scatterings of farming activity – mainly small stock farming of black-headed Dorper (reared for mutton) and Karakul, bred for their prized pelts. Karakul sheep have the unusual characteristic of storing fat in their tails, giving them a renowned ability to forage and thrive under extremely harsh living conditions. The species originated in Central Asia and was introduced to the region by German colonists in the early twentieth century.

The two major towns of the south are Lüderitz and Keetmanshoop. A small coastal town and thriving hub of the fishing industry, Lüderitz is situated on an infamously treacherous coastline and was the first German settlement in the then South West Africa. Today, even amongst the flurry of commerce, Lüderitz remains a charming and tranquil town, retaining its old-world charm through various fine examples of German colonial architecture. Nearby, visitors can experience the eerie surreal stillness of Kolmanskop, Namibia's most famous 'ghost town' with its iconic sand-filled *belle époque* era homes. Once a town of great opulence during the diamond rush, Kolmanskop was swiftly abandoned when the prospecting focus of the day moved elsewhere, leaving behind a fascinating insight of life at the turn of the twentieth century.

As the unofficial 'capital' of the south, the town of Keetmanshoop is the main centre of the scenic and historic attractions in the region. Founded in 1860 by the Rhenish Mission Society, the town still retains a quaint colonial feel with well-preserved original German buildings, as well as several dating back to the arrival of the first Europeans who journeyed across the Orange River to hunt, trade and explore the land.

Just north of Keetmanshoop is the ancient Quiver Tree Forest comprising approximately 250 specimens of *Aloe dichotoma*, a visually striking species of aloe known locally as a quiver tree (or *kokerboom* in Afrikaans), the oldest of which dates back almost three centuries. In the forest's surroundings another popular and dramatic site is a large area of precariously balanced dolerite rocks – known imaginatively as 'Giants' Playground'.

But of all the great attractions of the south, nothing quite captures the region's romance as the famed wild horses of the Namib, often spotted west of Aus, their manes flailing wildly in the wind as they gallop across the dusty barren desert landscape – a universally emotive symbol of freedom, passion and spirit.

Norotshama River Resort

ORANGE RIVER

Carving its way from the mountains of Lesotho to South Africa's Atlantic Ocean coast, the mighty Orange River flows through southern Namibia's Karas Region, creating a natural border between Namibia and South Africa, and providing much-needed relief to the arid, sun-scorched region.

At first glance much of Namibia's beautiful landscapes can appear unforgivingly barren, but surprises await at every turn and a closer look is always met with astonishing examples of life. Aussenkehr Valley is one of Namibia's southernmost wonders.

Historically the isolated Aussenkehr Valley was a largely uninhabited area. Nomadic Nama tribes passed through the valley and, for a brief period following the discovery of Orange River diamonds, German settlers fruitlessly tried their hand at farming.

In 1988 Dusan Vasiljevic, a Yugoslavian fruit trader with great vision and daring ambition, acquired the Aussenkehr Valley Farm – land that received less than 50 millimetres of rainfall a year – with the intention to plant the first vineyards in the area. Namibia's mild coastal climate was perfect for growing table grapes for Europe at times of the year when they are most vulnerable to frost elsewhere in the world, and Vasiljevic knew of several grape varieties that thrive on high heat and low humidity.

Today the Aussenkehr Valley Farm, which boasts over 1 200 hectares of vineyards, is the leading exporter of early table grapes to markets such as Europe, the United Kingdom, Russia and the Far East, and is the largest early table grape production farm in the southern hemisphere.

Nestled in the heart of the Aussenkehr Grape Valley is the luxurious Norotshama River Resort, uniquely located between hectares of vineyards, rugged mountain peaks and the Orange River. Greeted with famous southern Namibian hospitality, guests are presented with a wide range of experiences: from river rafting to dining under the stars; rock climbing and cultural village excursions to catching a glimpse of the legendary Namib desert horses.

Aussenkehr Settlement

The success story of the Aussenkehr Valley Farm and its demanding table grape production schedule has resulted in some 28 per cent of Namibia's agricultural employment – approximately 8 000 workers. With the alluring prospect of work in this remote southern region, a nearby rural community began to develop and, over time, the settlement of Aussenkehr has grown substantially with a population estimated to be between 16 000 and 30 000.

Today the people of Aussenkehr not only benefit from the grape industry but also from many new jobs created by growing tourism in the area. Local training programmes have brought new and varied skills to the rural community and the Nature Park also provides work for artisans such as mechanics, electricians and plumbers. Aussenkehr Valley Farm has provided much support for the community and although not yet an officially recognised town, Aussenkehr's resources continue to grow. The settlement features a government clinic and a primary school, as well as a modern grocery store.

Despite the harsh living conditions – summer temperatures can reach 50 °C in the river valley – the dusty streets of Aussenkehr are buzzing with life: the laughter of playing children can be heard all around, brightly-dressed women socialise outside local stalls and men gather at barber shops, usually with a proud parade of the latest cellphones – an important connection to the outside world and an ubiquitous rural symbol of status.

From its source in the Khomas Highlands near Windhoek, the Fish River flows across semi-desert plains and through the spectacular Fish River Canyon to join the Orange (Gariep) River in the south. Created over millions of years by the relentless forces of nature, the Fish River Canyon is one of the world's greatest natural wonders. It is the largest canyon in Africa and only second in size in

the world to the Grand Canyon in Arizona. With rock as old as 3 000 million years, the Canyon is 550 metres deep in places and extends for 161 kilometres. An 86-kilometre hiking trail through the canyon allows outdoor enthusiasts to experience the grandeur of one of the oldest wilderness areas on earth.

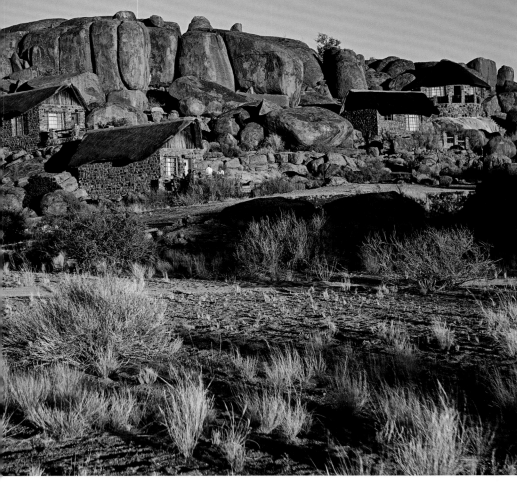

Canyon Lodge

GONDWANA CANYON PARK

A mere 20 kilometres from the Fish River Canyon, amidst a dramatic panorama of vast Nama Karoo plains, lies the extraordinary Gondwana Canyon Lodge. Built playfully in-and-amongst enormous granite boulders so characteristic of the area, the 25 natural-stone chalets blend almost magically with their ancient surrounds.

Over a century ago many of southern Namibia's game species were decimated by hunting or driven away by local farmers. The renowned and proactive Gondwana Collection was formed with a deeply committed philosophy to sustainable tourism in Namibia and in 1995 it acquired its first piece of land – an area of 1 260 square kilometres today known as the Gondwana Canyon Park. The park forms part of the Nama Karoo Desert and is the largest nature reserve in the collection, which includes three other southern Namibian regions.

Transforming the region into a nature conservation area, internal fences were removed, watering places suitable for game were set up and previously indigenous game species were reintroduced. Today, the Gondwana Canyon Park is unique in the region for its quantity and diversity of wildlife – animals such as springbok, oryx, red hartebeest, ostrich and mountain zebra thrive in the protected but nevertheless harsh terrain, and there are ever increasing sightings of leopard in the area.

The unusual main building of the Gondwana Canyon Lodge is the original early 1900s farmhouse built by Alfons Schanderl, a reservist from the colonial German forces – the Schutztruppe. Young men who volunteered for Schutztruppe service could look forward to farmland at special prices together with favourable start-up loans, and in 1908 the young Bavarian soldier purchased a 10 000-hectare piece of farmland called Karios. Shortly after, he was joined by his brother Stefan and the two set out to build the main farmhouse which, quite unlike any other found in Namibia, references the architectural style of their home village in upper Bavaria (some 70 kilometres east of Munich). Perched on the building's ridge is another old Bavarian tradition – an initial-bearing wrought-iron bed frame, most likely the handiwork of Alfons, a trained blacksmith. This curious custom notifies passing ladies that a bachelor resides on the property.

Kolmanskop

THE GHOST TOWN OF KOLMANSKOP

About 10 kilometres inland from Lüderitz lies Kolmanskop – an abandoned 'ghost town' from the diamond rush era. Kolmanskop has literally been overtaken by the sands of time and provides an eerie, surreal and fascinating insight into the life of diamond prospectors at the turn of the twentieth century.

Zacharias Lewala, a labourer employed by the Deutsche Kolonial Eisenbahnbau und Betriebsgesellschaft, discovered the first diamond in the area in April 1908. Thinking that it was merely an interesting looking stone, he gave his find to his supervisor, August Stauch, to add to his collection of local rocks. Instinctively curious, Stauch had it cleaned in an acid bath by a local doctor and travelled with it to Swakopmund where the stone was confirmed by a government geologist to be a diamond! Stauch swiftly (and wisely) proceeded to obtain prospecting licenses and peg claims in the area.

News spread fast of an area so rich in diamonds that they could literally be picked up off the ground and within weeks prospectors had settled in the area to claim their fortunes. Soon after, in September 1908, the German government declared the area and a large section around it as *Sperrgebiet* (forbidden territory) to protect the burgeoning diamond industry from the clutches of foreign mining companies, illegal prospectors and potential thieves. The restricted area (today known as Diamond Area 1) stretched from the Orange River to the 26th parallel, about 72 kilometres north of Lüderitz.

To attract skilled personnel to the remote, sandblown desert town and with fortunes having been made overnight, diamond mine owners created an environment of such luxury that it resembled the *belle époque* of pre-war Europe. A theatre and orchestra were established and opera and theatre companies brought out from Germany, and a casino and skittle club (*kegelbahn*) were also built. The local hospital, one of the country's finest, was the first in the southern hemisphere to have an x-ray machine. Despite these luxuries, Kolmanskop experienced difficulty in obtaining fresh, drinkable water and the settlement largely depended on barrelled water shipped from Cape Town.

Over 1 000 kilograms of diamonds were extracted at Kolmanskop before the First World War. Yields eventually began to wane and richer alluvial deposits were discovered at Oranjemund. In 1938 most of the mining equipment was redeployed at Oranjemund, but it was not until as late as 1956 that the last of the inhabitants finally left the settlement.

Abandoned but not forgotten, a section of the deserted town was restored in the 1980s by mining company CDM (now NamDeb) and a museum was established, giving Kolmanskop a new lease on life as a popular tourist attraction.

Klein Aus Vista

GONDWANA SPERRGEBIET RAND PARK

The Gondwana Sperrgebiet Rand Park covers 51 000 hectares and includes Namibia's 'Namaqualand' – the Succulent Karoo. Following the winter rains, the desert erupts in a dazzling spectacle of colours as it transforms into a carpet of flowers. This is the most bio-diverse desert on earth.

The myriad wonderments of Namibia's South can all be experienced close by to the popular Klein Aus Vista Ranch, whether on an extraordinary sunset drive or by hiking, jogging or mountain biking on marked trails through the wide and mountainous landscapes. Only a short drive away, one can also visit the harbour town of Lüderitz and experience the eerie windswept silence of Kolmanskop – Namibia's famous ghost town.

Set within a majestic backdrop where the Auas mountain escarpments meet desert plains and dunes, the estate of Klein Aus Vista is a place of palpable tranquility. Four distinctly different kinds of accommodation are on offer: *Desert Horse Inn* (*opposite and top right*), located in the Auas Mountains at 1 400 metres above sea level, affords grand vistas of mountain scenery and sweeping desert plains. A 15-minute drive further reveals the eight natural-rock *Eagle's Nest Chalets* (*bottom left*), nestled against a mountain slope, each set between massive granite boulders. Here the endless vistas are saturated with golden-red sunsets and one can find true solitude, silence and space. Those with a more adventurous appetite can set up camp amidst imposing old camelthorn trees at the *Desert Horse Campsite*, and for an exclusive experience, Klein Aus Vista's lone *Geisterschlucht Cabin* is a rustic treat, located in a picturesque and sheltered valley of the Auas Mountains.

As would be expected of Klein Aus Vista's *Geisterschlucht* (Ghost Valley), a good ghostly story awaits. Curiously out of place and time, a lone 1934 model Hudson Terraplane automobile, peppered with bullet holes and corroded by the searing desert heat, sits silently at the foot of a valley slope. This was the spot, as the story goes, where police caught up with two diamond thieves, on the

run from the Sperrgebiet (Diamond Restricted Area). The dramatic shoot out proved fatal for the two bandits, but the diamonds were never recovered. Ever since, locals have reported sightings of the two ghosts, haunting the valley on moonlit nights in search of their lost loot.

To catch a glimpse of Namibia's legendary wild horses, galloping freely through the vast sandy plains between Lüderitz and Aus, is nothing short of breathtaking. The wild horses of the Namib are amongst the few groups of feral horses in the world and the only in existence to have adapted to harsh desert conditions. Various theories surmise their mysterious origins – some believe they are

the descendants of horses left behind when the German Schutztruppe abandoned Aus during the South West African campaign in 1915, while another popular theory is that they are descendants of the horse stud belonging to Baron von Wolf, who built Duwisib Castle 160 kilometres north-east of Garub.

Lüderitz

The small coastal town of Lüderitz is characterised by bustling commerce, old-world charm and a most eventful history. It was the first German settlement in South West Africa – lured by tales of copper and other mineral deposits, Bremen tobacco merchant Franz Lüderitz purchased the bay, Angra Pequena, and the surrounding coastal area from Nama leader Joseph Fredericks. Shortly after, following an appeal to protect his Lüderitzland, Germany annexed the territory in 1884.

Almost four centuries earlier, in 1488, Portuguese explorer Bartolomeu Dias erected a three-metre, 360-kilogram limestone beacon (*padrão*) after he had succeeded in rounding the Cape of Good Hope. Last recorded as being seen in 1786 by the captain of the British HMS *Nautilus*, the original *padrão* was subsequently destroyed, most likely by treasure-hunting sailors. In 1855, a guano merchant seaman, Captain Carew, took the remaining fragments he could find to the South African Museum in Cape Town. On 25 July 1988, in commemoration of the 500th anniversary of the Dias landing, a replica of the *padrão*, carved from Namib dolemite by Karibib stonemason Paul Petzold, was erected on the original site.

Lüderitz lies on a treacherous coast and was generally avoided on the trade routes, but large numbers flocked to the harbour town during the 1843–1845 guano-harvesting rush. Known as 'white gold', guano was an important source of nitrates for gunpowder as well as a highly effective fertiliser due to its high phosphorus and nitrogen content and its relative lack of odour compared to other forms of organic fertiliser such as horse manure.

A brief spell of calm followed the guano rush until the famous diamond rush of the early 1900s, bringing thousands of hopeful prospectors to the area.

The quaint German atmosphere of Lüderitz is created by the many fine examples of colonial-style buildings, reflecting the Jugendstil architecture of the early 1900s. Perhaps its best-known example is Haus Goerke (*opposite, top left*) on the slopes of Diamantberg (Diamond Mountain), an imposing home built for Hans Goerke, the Inspector of Stores, during the area's diamond boom and

believed to be the work of German architect Otto Ertl. Today Lüderitz is a thriving fishing centre, most notably for pilchards, rock lobster and thriving oyster and abalone farms. The popular Lüderitz Waterfront (*above left*) forms an integral part of the harbour town's atmosphere and links the central business district to the Atlantic Ocean.

Desert Homestead & Horse Trails

Just over 30 kilometres south-east of Sesriem – the gateway to the dunes of Sossusvlei – lies the magical Desert Homestead. Pristine, silent and timeless, the 20 thatch-roofed chalets of the Desert Homestead are set in a vast, dramatic valley sheltered by the Nabib, Tsaris and Naukluft mountains, with majestic views reaching the distant red dunes of the Namib Desert in the west as well as the 'Table Mountain' of Namibia's south (*top left*).

The tranquil, rustic setting of the Desert Homestead is the perfect start to one of the many adventures on offer, most notably their popular horse trails – an exhilarating way to explore the expansive surrounding area and experience the true freedom of Namibia's wild landscapes.

Galloping unhindered into the unknown, wind rushing through your hair, the intoxicating smell of dry desert air – whether a novice or skilled rider, the experience of Namibia's open landscapes is enthralling. Sundowner rides present commanding views of rugged landscapes bathed in hues of pastel and longer 'sleep-out' excursions provide ample opportunities to explore – meandering across endless plains, discovering ancient watercourses and sleeping under crystal clear starry skies.

Riding in the grasslands surrounding the Desert Homestead one might catch a glimpse of the region's mysterious 'fairy circles' – bare circular patches with diameters between two and 15 metres that dot the landscape. How they are formed remains a mystery, baffling scientists for over 40 years. Unproved theories range from burrowing rodents to poisoning, from microscopic fungi to toxins left in the soil by euphorbias that once may have grown there. The Himba believe the circles are created by the spirits and the region's San tribes have ascribed spiritual and magical powers to them. Unsurprisingly, popular explanations include UFO landings and, of course, the magical night-time work of fairies.

SOSSUSVLEI & THE NAMIB-NAUKLUFT PARK

Proclaimed in 1979, the far-reaching Namib-Naukluft Park is an amalgamation of several areas into one national park. Three nature reserves were declared in 1907 by German Governor Friedrich von Lindequist, one being 'Game Reserve No. 3' in the central Namib Desert, which later became known as the Namib Desert Park. In 1979, the park merged with the Naukluft Mountain Zebra Park as well as unoccupied state land and was renamed the Namib-Naukluft Park. Subsequently the park's borders expanded to include further surrounding areas and today the colossal park, covering some 49 768 square kilometres is the largest conservation area in Namibia and the fourth largest in the world.

Travellers from around the globe are drawn to the park's most popular attraction – the simply breathtaking area of Sossusvlei, home to Namibia's iconic star-shaped, orange-hued and age-old sand dunes. Although technically Sossusvlei is a specific salt and clay pan area surrounded by high red dunes in the southern part of the Namib Desert, the name has also come to represent the surrounding dramatic dune desertscape. Sossusvlei is an endorheic drainage basin (without outflows) for the ephemeral Tsauchab River and its name is one part Nama (*sossus*, meaning 'dead end') and one part Afrikaans (*vlei* meaning 'marsh').

Sossusvlei dunes are visually arresting – amongst the highest in the world, many rise above 200 metres and some reach staggering heights, such as the Big Daddy dune (325 metres) or the nearby Big Mamma, both an enticing challenge for tourists to ascend. Dune 7 (388 metres) is indeed the highest dune on earth. Due to a high percentage of iron in the sand and consequent oxidisation, the scintillating colours of the area's sand range from pinks to oranges, with the older dunes being a more intense red. With striking contrast many are offset against dazzling white clay pans at their bases. Strong multi-directional winds, in particular the southwester, give the dunes of Sossusvlei their characteristically lyrical star shape.

The most photographed dune in the world, Dune 45, is an 80-metre-high dune with a curvaceous edge, creating a graphic contrast between vivid orange sand and near black shadow. Its name is derived from the fact that it lies 45 kilometres from Sesriem – the gateway to Sossusvlei – and its gentle incline makes it a popular dune for visitors to climb. About 60 kilometres on the other side of the Sesriem gate, along the road to Solitaire, one can find ancient red petrified dunes, solidified to rock over billions of years.

Despite the arid conditions of the area the Namib-Naukluft Park supports a surprisingly varied flora and fauna. Distinctive euphorbia, acacia, commiphora and aloe plants are found in the park's high plateau and mountainsides. Most are low, slow-growing species, inventively adapted to conserving water during the dry season. Deeper kloofs in the area provide permanent springs, resulting in more lush, broad-leaf species, including wild, cluster and sycamore figs as well as camelthorn, buffalo thorn, wild olive and shepherd's trees.

The park's popular Welwitschia Trail, accessed east of Swakopmund, leads visitors on a picturesque route, showcasing a unique botanical curiosity endemic to the Namib Desert – the *Welwitschia mirabilis*. One of the world's rarest plants, these 'living fossils' were described by Charles Darwin as the 'platypus of the plant kingdom', and have adapted remarkably to the hostile desert climate. Throughout its lifetime, the plant produces a single pair of leaves, which are unpalatable for animals. A magnificent specimen known as 'The Great Welwitschia' can be seen along the trail and is estimated to be over 1 500 years old.

A variety of wildlife is found throughout the Namib-Naukluft Park. Springbok, oryx and ostrich traverse the desert plains, while animals such as Hartmann's mountain zebra, klipspringer, baboon, leopard and African wild cat are found in the canyons of the Swakop and Kuiseb rivers.

But perhaps the most fascinating members of the Namib's wildlife are the smaller creatures – intriguingly adapted to survive in the seemingly inhospitable Namib dunes, and many of which are found nowhere else on the planet. More than 20 tenebrionid beetles (known locally as 'tok-tokkies' because of their distinctive mating sound) have adapted to the harsh desert conditions. Some dig water-collecting trenches, while others survive the searing heat with extra long legs, keeping them at a kinder distance from the hot sands while also allowing them to move at an extraordinary pace, producing a compassionately cooling wind. Curious lizards of the region include Skoog's lizard, a vegetarian reptile that dives in a corkscrew motion into the sand, and the shovel-snouted lizard, whose intriguing 'thermal dance' helps it to cope with the extreme heat radiating from dune surfaces.

Other endemic animals include Grant's golden mole and two gerbil species – Setzer's hairy-footed gerbil and the dune hairy-footed gerbil. Two endemic bird species are the dune lark, found in the sand dunes, and Gray's lark of the gravel plains, and high above the endless fauna-filled plains, Naukluft's steep cliffs are nesting grounds for various cliff-breeding bird species, including the majestic Verreaux's eagle.

Hoodia Desert Lodge

One of the region's best kept secrets, nestled on the banks of the Tsauchab River, is the breathtaking Hoodia Desert Lodge. Majestic mountains, glowing in purples and pinks as the sun sets, surround the luxury lodge which lies in a vast savannah landscape. Although covering a wide distance, Hoodia Desert Lodge is in fact indulgently intimate, with only 12 luxury en-suite partly-tented, thatch-roofed bungalows. The generous space between each allows guests to fully marvel in the experience of boundless open space – a rare luxury afforded by so few destinations.

The lodge takes its name from a group of succulent plants of the genus *Hoodia*, from the family Apocynaceae. For centuries the plants have been used by the San people as an ancient elixir for a variety of ills – a cure for abdominal cramps, indigestion and tuberculosis, a remedy for hypertension and diabetes and, most famously, as an appetite suppressant.

The lodge is family-owned and managed by charismatic couple Thomas and Henreza Becker, whose infectious passion about the area sets the tone for a journey of adventure and escapism. Henreza's innovative international and traditional cuisine accompanied by the lodge's wide, exclusive variety of vintage South African wines, is a much needed respite from the exploits of a Hoodia Lodge day – whether a full day Sossusvlei excursion discovering the towering dunes, dry lakes and desert-adapted flora and fauna, a hike through the Sesriem Canyon or a guided expedition into the Namib-Naukluft Mountains. And after dinner guests are treated to a spectacular show – a cavernous star-filled night sky to impress even the most experienced of stargazers.

Sesriem, the gateway to the famous red dunes of Sossusvlei, is a mere 20-minute drive away, making the lodge an ideal base for excursions in the area. As a welcome escape from the scorching midday sun, the Hoodia Lodge team set up legendary desert lunches for their guests under the shade of trees at the foot of the dunes, providing just about the most remarkable 'restaurant' setting that one can experience.

Sossus Dune Lodge

The only fixed accomodation within the park is Namibia Wildlife Resorts' exclusive Sossus Dune Lodge, a spectacular luxury lodge impressively placed at the foot of a craggy mountain, less than four kilometres from Sesriem gate and moments from the much-visited Sesriem Canyon. Raised wooden walkways link each of the lodge's 25 chalets – their design a modern twist on traditional Ovambo homes, with wooden frames, canvas walls and thatched roofs. Generously spaced across the peaceful plains, each room offers breath-taking views of the distant dunes to the west and some of Namibia's most remarkable orange- and purple-hued sunsets.

Being the Namib-Naukluft Park's exclusive lodge, guests are able to reach the imposing dunes of Sossusvlei before sunrise and stay until after sunset, experiencing a rare glimpse of Namibia's most famous dunes glowing intensely in the early and late sun's 'magic light'.

The second most visited tourist attraction after Sossusvlei is the Sesriem Canyon, just moments from the lodge. Although not comparable in size to the Fish River Canyon, Sesriem is indeed a spectacle of its own, about a kilometre long and up to 30 metres deep. A natural canyon, its formation began over 30 million years ago when much of Namibia was buried by desert sands up to 200 metres deep. Rivers formed that ran from the massive escarpment of the Naukluft and Zaris mountains to the east and, following prehistoric deluges, large amounts of sand, boulder debris and dissolved limestone were carried down from the highlands and deposited on the desert floor. The northern hemisphere's Ice Age, occurring some two million years ago, brought about a significant drop in sea levels, which led to an increased flow rate of the Tsauchab River. Over time the mighty torrents began to cut through the conglomerates and sandstone beds of the area, forming the remarkable canyon – and today the distinctive thick layers of sedimentary rock and conglomerates can still be seen whilst hiking through the canyon bed.

Arranged by nature's powerful forces, towering dunes encircle the barren Deadvlei, adjacent to Sossusvlei, in the Namib-Naukluft Park. Imprisoned in an amphitheatre of sand, the vlei has been permanently cut off from its former source of life: the Tsauchab River. Striking out from the central highlands, the river crawls westward until, about 70 kilometres from the coast, its efforts to reach the sea

are finally thwarted by a battalion of dunes. Once in a while, however, the river comes down in flood, creating a lush land of water and vegetation – an ephemeral haven that attracts animals and birds from afar. Although not petrified, the sun-blackened tree 'skeletons' do not decompose because of the area's extremely dry conditions. It is believed that Deadvlei's ancient trees are some 900 years old.

Dunes! Camera! Action!

Unsurprisingly, Namibia has become an increasingly popular destination for international film productions. Few locations on the planet can rival Namibia for the unique and diverse options on offer. Locations range from untouched beaches and vast salt pans to rugged mountains, deep canyons and spectacular desert landscapes – home to the world's highest sand dunes and largely uninhabited.

There are abandoned sand-filled ghost towns, colourful cosmopolitan cities and well-maintained pre-colonial German architecture, not to mention an abundance of wildlife and flora-filled savannah landscapes. Year-round filming is also made possible by Namibia's low rainfall – a great drawcard with an annual average of 325 days of sunshine!

Founded in 2000, the Swakopmund-based Namib Film is the country's leading film production service company and an omnipresent driving force behind the emerging industry's large-scale projects. Led by renowned executive producer Guy Nockels and his lively team, the company has overseen seemingly impossible requests and schedules, hosted some of the biggest music and movie stars, and helped to place Namibia firmly on the international production scene.

Namibia has a film-making heritage going back to the earliest days of cinematography, including Robert Lynn's Technicolor adventure *Coast of Skeletons*. Besides being a perennial favourite for wildlife documentaries, tourism filming and survival programmes, the local industry's cutting edge technology has attracted major Hollywood productions, such as *Beyond Borders* (starring Angelina Jolie and Clive Owen), *Flight of the Phoenix* (starring Dennis Quaid), Walt Disney's *Young Black Stallion* and the post-apocalyptic *Mad Max: Fury Road* (starring Tom Hardy and Charlize Theron).

Bollywood also produces many feature films in Namibia, including *Dhoom 2* and *Ghajini*, one of the highest grossing Bollywood films of all time.

Eighty-three kilometres from Sossusvlei's entrance, more or less 'in the middle of nowhere', travellers encounter the fantastical hamlet of Solitaire. A narrow, dusty road in an otherwise barren landscape is strewn with corroded time-worn automobiles, leading to a 'last chance' gas station and general dealer amidst cacti, memorabilia and Africa's most famous apple pie.

Larger-than-life Scotsman Moose McGregor bakes piping hot treats daily at his most unlikely desert bakery. His wares have become the stuff of legend, most notably the apple pie, for which travellers from around the world have made pilgrimage. Ask for cream with your apple pie and you'll receive Moose's standard retort – 'it's our cow's day of rest!'

Solitaire Guest Farm Desert Ranch

With breathtaking views over the vast Namib desertscape and impressive Naukluft Mountains, the Solitaire Guest Farm Desert Ranch is a place of pristine serenity, just moments away from the famous Solitaire gas station.

The privately owned guest farm opened its doors in 2004 promoting conservation sustained through low impact eco-tourism – a vision shared by owners Walter and Simone Swarts and renowned explorer, adventurer and geophysicist Pasquale Scatturo. As part of this vision a partnership was formed with the N/a'an ku sê foundation and the land was made available for the Namib Carnivore Conservation Centre, which opened in June 2011. Here large carnivores are rehabilitated and wildlife is monitored and researched. Two wildlife biologists are stationed at the ranch and guests can accompany them on educational and thrilling cheetah tracking safaris.

A stay at the Solitaire Guest Farm Desert Ranch is always lively, whether staying in one of the rooms of the original 1950s farmhouse, the private thatched luxury chalet at the base of the mountains or pitching a tent at the ranch's picturesque campsite.

In 1948 Willem Christoffel van Coller bought 33 000 hectares of undeveloped land from the South West Administration for the purpose of farming Karakul sheep. His wife, schoolteacher Elsie Sophia van Coller, came up with the name Solitaire – a word meaning single set diamond as well as a place of solitude. This, she felt, was the perfect name for a place both solitary and precious.

Besides the wildlife in the surrounding plains, the Solitaire Guest Farm is filled with its own colourful characters – delightful meerkats scurry about the farm looking for food or basking in front of the fire on cold mornings, Bokkie the rescued springbok, Max, a rehabilitated oryx, and a host of canine characters greet guests on arrival and to say goodnight and Sammy the African grey parrot is often heard to chirp 'lekker slaap' (Afrikaans for 'sleep well').

Namibia's Cheetahs

Namibia is home to the world's largest cheetah population. For thousands of years the elegant feline has inspired man with its graceful agility and astounding speed. Deified by the ancient Egyptians, pharaohs kept cheetahs as close personal companions and believed they had the power to swiftly carry their souls to the afterlife. The sixteenth-century Indian Mogul, Akbar the Great, kept over 9 000 cheetahs during his 49 year reign, each of their details carefully recorded.

A wide variety of cheetah once roamed the plains and savannahs of Africa, Asia, Europe and North America. Over thousands of years, dramatic changes in climate drastically reduced their numbers, leaving all species of cheetah extinct except for *Acinonyx jubatus*, today the sole member of its genus.

Famed for their speed, cheetahs are the world's fastest land animal, able to reach speeds of 112 kilometres per hour and accelerate from zero to 60 kilometres per hour in just three long-limbed strides. With such an exceptional aptitude, cheetahs are unsurprisingly the most specialised member of the cat family. Endowed with a powerful heart, oversized liver, and large, robust arteries, its long, slender legs and narrow, lightweight body are the ultimate aerodynamic combination. Its hip and shoulder girdles swivel on a flexible spine, giving greater reach to the legs, while the cheetah's muscular, lengthy tail acts as a stabiliser, counteracting its body weight. During a high-speed chase, the cheetah's respiratory rate climbs from 60 to 150 breaths per minute with only one foot at a time touching the ground (except for two points during its 7–8-metre stride when no feet touch the ground) and after approximately 600 yards it slows down, exhausted and dangerously vulnerable to other predators.

The cheetah, which is often mistaken for leopard, has various distinct markings, particularly the long, dark teardrop lines from the corner of its eyes to its mouth, and the solid oval spots on its slender, elongated and tan-coloured body.

Cheetahs are a protected species in Namibia, however their survival as a species faces many challenges – a rapid decline in numbers has resulted in genetic inbreeding, leading to greater susceptibility to disease, and with the majority of Namibia's cheetah being found on commercial farms, their threat as a livestock predator has resulted in many being killed by farmers.

Between 10 000 and 12 500 cheetahs are estimated to remain in 24 to 26 African countries and less than 100 animals in Iran. Today some 3 000 free-ranging cheetahs can be found in Namibia.

Bagatelle

KALAHARI GAME RANCH

Characterised by brilliant saturated red sand dunes and golden grass savannah, much of eastern and southern Namibia is dominated by the ancient expansive Kalahari Desert. The Kalahari Desert, or Kgalagadi as it is known in some areas, stretches over 900 000 square kilometres across seven countries – Botswana, Zambia, South Africa, Zimbabwe, Namibia, Angola and the Democratic Republic of Congo. Unlike the Namib Desert to the west, the Kalahari is technically a semi-desert, receiving considerably more rainfall. Its porous, sandy soils, however, are unable to effectively retain surface water. The result of the differing climate is a pristine wilderness with luxuriant grass cover after good rains, glowing orange dunes and a wide array of wildlife and plant life.

The Namibian area of the Kalahari Desert is covered with trees, ephemeral rivers and fossil watercourses that allow large numbers of mammals, birds, reptiles and amphibians, plant life and insects to thrive. The landscape is typically dotted with camelthorn, red ebony and other acacias, and the extensive array of wildlife includes cheetah (for which the Kalahari's grass provides perfect ambush cover), springbok, oryx and giraffe as well as smaller animals such as meerkat, honey badger and yellow mongoose. Birdlife is also abundant in the Kalahari's cobalt blue skies, particularly large raptors such as the majestic martial eagle, brown snake eagle and lappet-faced vulture.

Amidst this magical environment of scintillating orange dunes and pristine wilderness is the renowned Bagatelle Kalahari Game Ranch, situated on the edge of the southern Kalahari in the mixed tree and shrub savannah. The luxurious chalets of Bagatelle (a French word meaning 'something small and insignificant') are humbled only by the unparalleled views to the south-west, powerfully illustrating the sheer vastness and beauty unique to the region. Some chalets sit proudly on wooden stilts atop commanding sand dunes while others, made of 600 millimetre-thick hay bales, are nestled in the valleys (or 'dune streets') between the sandy dunes. This is the spirit of Africa at its best!

In association with the Cheetah Conservation Fund, the lodge are custodians of rehabilitated cheetah unable to be released into the wild. Their exceptional cheetah facilities, with a strong focus on conservation and education, are amongst the finest in the country and allow guests to observe these speedy felines at play – in particular Pepper, a beautiful female cheetah that has naturally become the ranch's much-admired mascot.

WINDHOEK

Namibia's rainbow capital

Much of Namibia is characterised by vast, endless plains showcasing the country's ancient formations in pristine, largely uninhabited settings. It is a land famous for 'contrasts', generally with reference to the stunning contrasts of nature, dramatically juxtaposed throughout the country. But perhaps the most delightful contrast to the rest of the country is the lively, bright, bustling, typically African, typically German, historical, modern city of Windhoek, fittingly Namibia's capital. Windhoek is Namibia's largest city and is situated at the country's epicentre, around 1 680 metres above sea level in the Khomas Highland plateau area. It is surrounded by the Auas Mountains in the south-east, the Eros Mountains in the north-east and the Khomas Hochland in the west.

The busy city thrums with activity, playing the country's social, economic and cultural centre. Its population of approximately 340 000 is on the continual increase and visitors stream into the city each day from the two local airports – Hosea Kutako International (handling over 400 000 passengers a year) and Eros Airport (the country's busiest with around 12 000 individual flights each year).

Windhoek is the most popular starting point for those beginning a Namibian journey of discovery and its seamless blend of history and modernity, as well as its harmonious mix of cultures, make it a perfect introduction to the country.

The ever-busy Independence Avenue, lined with open-air German cafés, local Afro-cuisine restaurants, crafts and souvenir shops and hawkers selling their traditional wares, runs through the heart of downtown Windhoek. The tempo and sounds are distinctly that of a modern African city, while an equally strong 'continental' atmosphere is created by the city's many historical buildings dating back to the days of German colonial rule.

Situated along Independence Avenue is Zoo Park, a landscaped public park with a large pond, tall shade trees, a children's playground and an open-air theatre, providing a focal point for social life in the city. Within the park is a column designed by Namibian sculptor Dörthe Berner that commemorates a Stone Age elephant hunt that occurred here some 5 000 years ago. In the early 1960s a dramatic discovery was made of the remains of two elephants and several quartz tools used to cut up the carcasses.

Just to the west of Zoo Park, one of the city's most striking and recognisable landmarks is the Christuskirche (*left*), standing proudly in the historic centre of Windhoek. The oldest Evangelical Lutheran church in Namibia, it was officially consecrated on 16 October 1910, following a decade of building delays due to the Herero and Nama uprisings against German colonial rule. Its neo-Romanesque-style architecture mixed with Art Nouveau elements was designed by German government architect Gottlieb Redecker and the church was constructed primarily of quartz sandstone mined at Guche-Ganus Farm in the vicinity of present Avis Dam. International elements are also found throughout the church – the portal and altar are made of Carrara marble from Italy, the clock, three bronze bells and sections of the roof were shipped from Germany and the colourful stained-glass windows in the sanctuary were a gift from Emperor Wilhelm II. Christuskirche was proclaimed a national monument on 29 November 1974.

Windhoek is filled with historical monuments celebrating, remembering and memorialising the many milestones of the country's colourful history. The emotive Heroes' Acre on the outskirts of Windhoek commemorates Namibia's freedom struggle, while older memorials such as The Cross of Sacrifice, opposite the military cemetery on Robert Mugabe Avenue, honours soldiers lost on both sides of the two world wars. The Oudstryders Memorial in Bismarck Street was erected in memory of the Boer Bittereinders, Afrikaner trekboers who moved to German South West Africa to escape living under British rule in South Africa. One of the most prominent landmarks in Windhoek is the Reiter Denkmal, more commonly known as the Equestrian Memorial. Commemorating the lives lost during the Herero and Nama rebellions between 1904 and 1908, the bronze mounted soldier has been moved from its position near the Parliament Buildings to stand sentry in front of Alte Feste, an historical fortress built in 1890 that today houses the National Museum.

There are various theories as to how Windhoek acquired its name. Literal translation from Afrikaans is 'wind corner', however this is most likely co-incidental given the fact that the area has never been particularly windy. The most popular theory is that the celebrated Nama captain, Jonker Afrikaner, who settled in the area in the early 1840s, named the city after the Winterhoek Mountains of his homeland in South Africa's Cape. Previous names included / Ai // Gams, a Nama word meaning 'firewater' and referring to the area's hot springs (the unusual punctuation indicates the distinguishing Nama click sounds), and Otjomuise, a Herero word meaning 'the place of steam'. Rhenish missionaries called it Elberfeld, Wesleyan missionaries called it Concordiaville and, in 1837, visiting British explorer Sir James Alexander proposed Queen Adelaide's Bath in honour of his queen.

Situated on the outskirts of Windhoek is Namibia's largest and most elaborate post-independence monument, the emotionally-charged Heroes' Acre (*right*). Inaugurated in 2002, the memorial stands in remembrance of those who contributed to the fight for Namibia's independence. With a sizeable marble obelisk and a bronze statue of the Unknown Soldier at its centre, the site contains

parade grounds and a grandstand for 5 000 people, as well as a burial site consisting of 174 tombs. National heroes memorialised with tombstones include Hendrik Witbooi, king of the Nama people, and Kahimemua Nguvauva, Chief of the Ovambanderu. Another equally powerful monument dedicated is the 40-metre-high Independence Memorial Museum (*left*) built next to the Alte Feste.

Windhoek's streets are filled with optimism and buzz – fashionable youth add splashes of colour with their Afro-chic sensibilities as they pass Herero women dressed in their striking traditional attire. Executives rush to their next meeting, adeptly weaving through sidewalk craftsmen displaying African drums and woodcarvings from the north – all to a soundtrack of animated cellphone chatter and street-

corner African pop, with loudspeaker DJs promoting deals on short-term finance. Enticing smells waft from the many bakeries, cafés and restaurants throughout the city. A wide variety of cuisine is on offer, from street-stall quick bites to sophisticated European fare, such as The Gourmet Restaurant (*above left*), a perennial favourite with its palm-treed courtyard next to the African Street Market.

Tintenpalast & The State House

The imposing buildings set amongst lush manicured gardens and tall palm trees just north of Robert Mugabe Avenue were designed at the turn of the twentieth century by Gottlieb Redecker, the architect responsible for the Christuskirche built nearby. Completed in November 1913, the buildings were known as Tintenpalast, or 'Ink Palace', alluding to the ink that flowed on the extensive paperwork generated there during the time the buildings served as administrative headquarters of the German colonial government. The buildings were renovated shortly after the country gained independence in 1990, and today they are the stately and gracious home of Namibia's Parliament.

Nearby to the Parliament Gardens is the original State House, located on Robert Mugabe Avenue. Much needed expansions were not possible due to the building's central location and today it has become the residence and office of Namibia's Prime Minister. In September 2002, at the end of founding President Sam Nujoma's illustrious term of office, construction began on a new State House, located in the Auasblick suburb of Windhoek. Following 66 months of design and construction by the North Korean Mansudae Overseas Projects, the new imposing, grand and ultra-modern State House (*following page*) was unveiled to great admiration.

The State House of the Republic of Namibia is the administrative capital of Namibia, as well as the official residence of the President of Namibia. The site covers 25 hectares and is enclosed by a two-kilometre-long steel fence. The administrative area consists of the Office of the President, the offices of cabinet members and 200 staff offices of the president. There are two apartments and a guesthouse for visiting heads of state, twin helipads opposite the main gate and beautiful park-like grounds with stately copper animal replicas. The sumptuous interiors are decorated with impressive large-scale artworks showcasing the country's natural beauty, history, people and politics – these include a bold wood carving representing women from all ethnic groups in the country, a dramatic painting of the majestic Epupa Falls, and a powerful entrance hall artwork depicting the members of the first Namibian cabinet, including first President Dr Sam Nujoma, His Excellency Dr Hifikepunye Pohamba, Hage Geingob, Theo-Ben Gurirab, Ben Amathila, Libertina Amathila, Hidipo Hamutenya and Gert Hanekom.

Hilton Windhoek

FIVE-STAR WINDHOEK LUXURY

Since its humble beginnings in 1919, Hilton Hotels have become the most recognised name in the hospitality industry, synonymous with the idea of the luxury hotel and remaining a stylish, forward-thinking global leader. Hilton Hotels were the first to install televisions in guest rooms and more recently the first to earn both LEED and Green Seal environmental certifications. Their ever-increasing global expansion now encompasses over 3 900 hotels in 91 countries.

In 2011, Hilton Windhoek, the area's first five-star hotel, became the latest addition to Windhoek's skyline. Unveiled by His Excellency President Hifikepunye Pohamba, the remarkable ultra-modern monolith scintillating with thousands of glass panels, towers nine stories high above the city from its central downtown location. Situated between the Supreme Court, Windhoek Municipal buildings and Independence Avenue, the hotel is moments away from the city's CBD, government and historical buildings and tourist attractions.

Owned by the United Africa Group and operated by Hilton Worldwide, the hotel offers an unparalleled level of service and a dazzling array of amenities to impress the most travelled of jet-setters. The extensive luxurious accommodation includes four diplomatic suites, four king executive guest rooms, eight king deluxe rooms, 22 executive rooms, 12 double rooms, 99 king rooms and a tower-topping Presidential Suite, complete with dining room, living room, kitchen, state-of-the-art amenities and an unrivalled commanding view over the city.

The hotel's wide range of restaurants include show-kitchen dining with Namibian specialities prepared from a meat-aging cabinet, a notable collection of international wines from a contemporary glass wine cellar and private dining for up to 25 people. There is also a chic café with a tree-shaded decked terrace overlooking the bustling city (to a tinkling live piano soundtrack) and a vibrant sports bar. World-class conference facilities can accommodate every corporate whim from fully catered seminars of 250 people to late-night meetings in the 24-hour business centre. The hotel's ninth floor opens onto a rooftop paradise complete with crisp-white day beds, an 18-metre lap pool, state-of-the-art gym, luxury spa and exquisite panoramic views of the city below. As the sun sets over Namibia's capital, international travellers and the local who's who meet for cocktails at the city's trendiest night-time haunt – the glamorous Sky Bar – located at the far end of the ninth floor with views over the city skyline and to the mountains beyond.

Wecke & Voigts

ESTABLISHED 1892

Situated in the heart of Windhoek's Independence Avenue is the country's leading department store, Wecke & Voigts. Famed equally for its high-quality products as it is for its legendary history, the much-celebrated store has been trading since 1892 and still remains a family-run business, now in its fourth generation.

Gustav Voigts was one of the first German settler farmers in the former German colony of the then South West Africa and in 1910 became Windhoek's second Mayor. Gustav and his brothers Albert and Richard, originally from Meerdorf near Braunschweig in northern Germany, arrived on the continent in the late 1800s to take up a job offered by fellow-countryman Fritz Wecke, a merchant in the Boer Republic of Transvaal. From 1892 they began trading goods such as spades, buckets and saucepans with the Herero in exchange for cattle, which they subsequently sold to merchants in South Africa. These first dealings between German merchants and the leaders of the Herero (most notably Chiefs Samuel Maharero and Asser Riarua) were handled with great mutual respect and during the 1904 Herero uprising the Wecke & Voigts trading store was spared due to their longstanding relationship with the Herero people. Through sheer determination, respectful business principles and innovation (in 1972 they had the first air-conditioned store in the country), Wecke & Voigts grew to become one of Namibia's most respected businesses and the brothers' stories became the stuff of legend.

Today Wecke & Voigts stock fragrances, clothing, souvenirs, gifts, bathroom, kitchen and household accessories, and have a hugely popular in-house coffee shop at their flagship Independence Avenue store. The business has expanded to include the popular Hochland Spar and Maerua Superspar, as well as the prominent Wecke & Voigts National Wholesale, and after over 120 years of trading in Namibia, their proud slogan still reads '100% Namibian since 1892'.

Hotel Heinitzburg

ESTABLISHED 1914

Reminiscent of a medieval fairytale world, the wonderful German castle Heinitzburg is a romantic colonial relic.

The castle is built on a prime site on the apex of a hill overlooking Windhoek, the capital of Namibia, on the south-west coast of Africa.

Castle Heinitzburg was conceived and commissioned by Count von Schwerin for his fiancée Margarethe von Heinitz in 1914 as a token of his love for her. The continuity of elegance and charm of the castle has been lovingly perpetuated by the Raith family and continues to bring joy to all who come to stay here.

The castle is surrounded by the Auas Mountains in the south, the Eros Mountains in the east, and the Khomas Hochland in the west and has spectacular commanding views. Whether enjoying meals, coffee and pastries or a sundowner on the Garden Terrace, relaxing in the tranquil garden, cooling off at the sparkling pool after a sun-drenched day or fine dining at *Leo's at the Castle* with gourmet dishes by renowned Chef Tibor Raith, one is always assured a spectacular view and a perfect blend of African ambiance and traditional European standards of the highest order.

The elegant décor of each of the castle's 16 rooms is completely different to each other and reflects the reputation for meticulous attention to detail and comfort for which the Castle Heinitzburg management and staff are renowned. Heinitzburg is in constant demand for private functions and important corporate lunches and dinners. These can be held in one of their special rooms in the original castle, such as the elegant gourmet dining room *Leo's at the Castle*, the exclusive private venue *Knight's Room*, or the extraordinary and intimate dining area in the *Wine Cellar*, which is excavated into the mountain rock and boasts the largest collection of carefully selected South African wines in Namibia.

The legendary Joe's Beerhouse

A restaurant unlike any other on the continent – Joe's Beerhouse is a popular Namibian tourist attraction, a must-do activity for locals (weekly) and for any tourist passing through Windhoek. For travellers on the way 'in', a pre-adventure drink at Joe's is tradition, plans are made, stories, tips and tales are shared by locals and the Namibian spirit of adventure is vividly brought to life. As strong a tradition is a second visit to Joe's for those on the way 'out', a dinner filled with excitable post-adventure recollections, stories shared from along the way and a final taste of ice-cold Namibian draft…until the next time.

Joe's Beerhouse, known as 'The most famous Beerhouse on the African continent', is a truly Namibian restaurant on a grand scale. With 107 employees and a capacity to seat over 460 guests, the mega-restaurant is divided into various areas including three thatched bars, a lapa, beer garden and an outside boma with a fireplace. A non-stop stream of patrons fill the lively restaurant and its jam-packed bar – here you will find every kind of Namibian 'character' and conversations flow as easily as the Jägermeister. Those who have yet to experience a shot of Jägermeister will no doubt be introduced to several at Joe's – the German *Kräuterlikör* (herbal liqueur) made with 56 herbs and spices is a perennial favourite and tongue-in-cheek referred to as the restaurant's 'house wine' – unsurprising as Joe's Beerhouse serves more Jägermeister than any other establishment in Namibia.

New owners of Joe's Beerhouse, Manfred Enus and well-known restaurateur couple Carol-Jean and Thomas Rechter, have added their own stamp to the big personality eatery while still maintaining its original charm and allure, and upholding Joe's inimitable spirit and style. Every inch of Joe's Beerhouse is filled to the brim with relics, old and new, collected by Joe on his legendary adventures across the country. Some quirky, some intriguing, some bizarre, each has a unique story to tell. Popular items include the trophy of two kudu bulls, their twisted horns intertwined for eternity, a pair of ox horns impossibly large in size, and a well-travelled roof-top Mini Cooper that had journeyed from Lisbon to Namibia – how did that get there? You'll have to order another round…

BEER

UGLY

Tragödie
am Seeis - Rivier - Mai 1958.
gefunden von:
Herrn W. Schiwon - Richthof
Seeis.

I NEVER DRINK ANYTHING STRONGER THAN GIN BEFORE BREAKFAST

Jägermeister
Europas großer Kräuterlikör
HERB-LIQUEUR
Produced and bottled by
MAST-JÄGERMEISTER AG
Wolfenbüttel, Germany

SERVE COLD - KEEP ON ICE

Jägermeister

BOTTLE WASSER

Chubb

I ALWAYS CARRY A LITTLE WHISKEY WITH ME
IN CASE I SEE A SNAKE
I ALWAYS CARRY A SNAKE AS WELL

River Crossing Lodge

Nestled amongst the foothills of the Auas Mountains, surrounded my majestic views over the Papageien Mountains, Camel Mountain and Moltkeblick (the second highest point in Namibia), River Crossing Lodge is a place of true tranquility, natural beauty, and astonishingly just five minutes from the heart of Windhoek. The short journey to the lodge starts by crossing the Klein Windhoek River (hence the lodge's name) before descending a winding gravel road, each twist and turn taking you further from the bustle of Namibia's busiest city and closer to the calm of pristine secluded nature.

The enchanting lodge with its pitched corrugated roofs and wide balconies harks back to German farm life in a bygone era. Whether enjoying a sundowner on the elevated wooden deck, relaxing (or swimming lengths) in the lengthy 17-metre swimming pool or surveying the landscape from one of the chalets, the sounds of mountain-top silence is palpable and the views unrivalled. Some of the chalets offer fairytale views over Windhoek while others face east, looking onto the stately Moltkeblick Mountains.

The lodge is set amidst a 6 500-hectare game reserve with varied flora and abundant wildlife, and there are a variety of options for exploring the many intriguing trails, from game drives to guided hikes to mountain biking. Increasingly popular are the nature horse rides, providing a quiet, non-invasive and eco-friendly way to explore the land while also allowing guests to get closer to the game than from a vehicle. Nineteen prime wildlife species are found on the reserve, including giraffe, wildebeest, roan and sable, as well as the occasional leopard and cheetah.

Midgard
Country Estate

OTJIHAVERA MOUNTAINS

The word 'Midgard' is found in Old Norse, Middle English and High German languages and refers to a paradise where the earth is reborn, fertile and green – a safe 'empire' for the people.

Midgard Country Estate is the result of one of the country's most famous 'empires', that of Carl List, founder of Namibia Breweries and conglomerate Ohlthaver & List. Young German bankers Carl List and Hermann Ohlthaver arrived in South West Africa in 1905 and in 1920 they risked their combined life savings on purchasing four small local breweries. Before long their fortunes amassed, having created one of Namibia's most successful companies (their 'Windhoek' lager still today being a source of national pride) and in 1937 Carl List acquired the Midgard and Okatjemise farms as a private country home. His son and successor, Carl Werner List, originally farmed the 12 000-hectare estate and transformed it into a fantastical wonderland – a playground for his fertile imagination, eccentric collections and a place of great adventure for his international society guests.

Today the unique farm, nestled in the unspoilt splendour of the Otjihavera Mountains about an hour's drive from Windhoek, operates as an immensely popular country estate and conference venue, allowing guests to experience the legendary property first-hand.

Every turn at the Midgard Country Estate reveals a delight – from the private *Kegelbahn* (nine pin skittle alley) to the life-size outdoor chess set; the antique train cart and vintage car collection to the impressive amphitheater complete with a full theatrical stage, curtains, backdrops and seating for up to 450 people. These are just some of the estate's wonders, all spaciously situated in a vast, sprawling country garden bordering the banks of the Swakop River as it meanders through the estate on its way to the Atlantic Ocean at Swakopmund. Apart from the myriad activities on offer (hiking and mountain trails, driving along 4x4 tracks, volley ball, tennis or dreamy late-night stargazing), particularly popular amongst guests are morning and afternoon game drives through the separate 2 000-hectare nature reserve along the Swakop River. Wildlife found here includes giraffe, blue and black wildebeest, oryx, kudu, hartebeest, eland, warthog, baboons, and smaller antelope species such as steenbok.

Erindi Private Game Reserve

NAMIBIA'S PRISTINE WILDLIFE EXPERIENCE

Forty kilometres east of the town of Omaruru, between the Erongo Mountain Nature Conservancy and the Omataku Mountains, stretching over an immense 70 000 hectares of varied landscapes ranging from mountains and bush to open grassland savannah as far as the eye can see, Erindi Private Game Reserve is one of the largest privately owned game reserves on the continent.

Some years ago the area of Erindi was an over-stocked, over-grazed cattle farm, later becoming a hunting enterprise with electrified game fences. Entrepreneurial visionaries and passionate conservationists, owners Gert Joubert and his nephew Paul phased out cattle farming entirely in an effort to resuscitate the damaged natural vegetation and large numbers of wildlife were reintroduced to the area. Hunting was transformed into a nature conservation venture, which after years of neglect was no mean feat. The trust of previously threatened animals had to be gradually regained and the delicate ecological balance between vegetation, herbivores and predators restored. Today the pioneering conservation programmes and eco-management models used in the restoration of local wildlife to Erindi Game Reserve is considered one of the great success stories of the country and Erindi continues to constantly implement and monitor programmes across all aspects of the land rehabilitation process.

Today, over 15 000 head of game teem freely over the large Erindi Game Reserve, including rare and highly endangered species such as African wild dog (*Lycaon pictus*) and Namibia's largest protected population of black rhinoceros (*Diceros bicornis*). Healthy populations of lion, cheetah and leopard as well as the rare brown hyaena (*Hyeana brunnea*) give Erindi a predator diversity matched by few other wildlife destinations. Guests can also expect to see elephant, giraffe, hippopotamus, waterbuck, crocodile, spotted hyaena, honey badger, small-spotted genet, serval, bat-eared fox, African wild cat, Hartmann's and Burchell's zebra, oryx, kudu, eland, springbok, blue and black wildebeest, impala, red hartebeest, Damara dik-dik, steenbok, duiker, klipspringer, ostrich, warthog and baboon.

The property's luxurious accommodation is set around the Old Trader's Lodge, where a broad viewing deck (as well as the surrounding 35 lavishly-appointed rooms) overlooks a dramatic floodlit waterhole filled with a constant hive of activity, from a variety of game moving along its banks to an abundance of cavorting hippo and crocodiles.

The hefty hippopotamus is amongst the largest living mammals on the planet, its weight exceeded only by elephants, rhinoceroses and whales. Males can reach up to 3 200 kilograms, although the heaviest known hippopotamus weighed close to 4 500 kilograms. The name hippopotamus is derived from ancient Greek for 'river horse', although its closest relatives are cetaceans, such as whales and porpoises.

Hippos do not have sweat glands and keep cool during the day by submerging themselves in water and wallowing in river-side mud. They do, however, produce a red glandular secretion that scatters light and absorbs ultraviolet rays – the hippos' own natural sun block! Baby hippos are born underwater at a weight between 25 and 45 kilograms and must swim to the surface to take their first breath.

Roidina
Nature Farm

OMARURU

Set in the vast Erongo Mountains highlands, where the plains of the savannah bushveld unite with the surrounding mountains and river valleys, is Roidina Nature Farm, a place of undeniable spiritual resonance amidst 5 000 acres of pristine natural wilderness.

More than simply a 'stop along the way' Roidina Nature Farm is a spiritual sanctuary – a life-changing experience for those seeking a calmness amongst the wide-open spaces of nature. Thomas and Inge Mausberg arrived in Namibia from Germany to pursue an industrial factory development project and during their stay established a deep connection with the country. The two began to dream of a nature farm where they could experience a different pace of life and share their passions with others. Roidina Nature Farm was opened in 2008 by Thomas and Inge – the farm's guardians – and before long they realised why they had been led to this place. The area is filled with an abundance of two crystal types – both believed to be powerful in their healing properties: rose quartz (often referred to as the 'love stone' due to its heart-chakra-opening energetic hallmark of unconditional love) and black tourmaline (known for its ability to repel negative energy, allowing for enhanced confidence and increased inspiration).

Once guests are suitably calmed by the pristine silence, gorgeous surroundings and sumptuous food, Roidina offers a host of soul-enriching experiences from bush walks and game drives (the farm is part of a 60 000-hectare conservancy with wildlife such as oryx, waterbuck, mountain zebra and cheetah) to unique Roidina horse-rides through the surrounding countryside where meaningful bonds are forged between rider and horse. For the ultimate in zen tranquility, a steep mountainous trail leads to Roidina's mountain chalet – a single rustic chalet perched on a 1 600-metre-high cliff, complete with the magical silence of remoteness and an unparalleled 360-degree panoramic view of the Namibian savannah below.

Foraging throughout the desert, the adorable meerkat, also known as a suricate, is a small mammal belonging to the mongoose family, and commonly found in many regions of southern Africa. When digging for small insects and scorpions, meerkats typically gather in groups (known as 'mobs') with one upright sentry on guard watching for predators.

The unmistakable giraffe, with its long neck and legs, horn-like ossicones and distinctive coat patterns, has intrigued many cultures, both ancient and modern. As the tallest living terrestrial animal and the largest ruminant, giraffes are able to feed on leaves at heights of up to 4.5 metres. Despite the length of its neck, a giraffe has only seven neck bones – the same number as a human.

Omaruru

THE GREEN JEWEL ON THE DESERT'S EDGE

Most of the 3 480 kilometres driven through Namibia to produce this book was done in a 4x4 with an 'OM' registration (Omaruru is the proud home of Project's & Promotions, HOBERMAN's distributor and Namibian head office) and, without fail, at each stop along the way locals from each region, whether in the remote deep south, bustling city centres or vast Caprivian savannah, looked at the licence plate, then the driver, smiled broadly and said slowly with a nod of approval 'Om-a-ru-ru!'

Omaruru, situated near the Erongo Mountains, on the usually dry ephemeral Omaruru River, is a small town with a big heart that continues to inspire Namibians and visitors alike with its colourfully inimitable mix of artists, artisans and dreamers on the desert's edge.

The several permanent springs in and around Omaruru were once home to the area's first artists – ancient San tribes whose rich rock art made thousands of years ago remain as testament to their activities in the region. Later, in the 1800s, the Herero tribe used Omaruru and the surrounding area for cattle grazing – the name Omaruru is derived from the Otjiherero language, meaning 'bitter milk', referring to the bitter taste of the cattle's milk after grazing on a certain shrub variety that grew at the springs. The town's first permanent houses, many of which are still standing today, were built by Swedish big game hunters around 1870, who within a few years eliminated much of the local wildlife, including elephant, black rhino and lion. Thanks to inspired local conservation efforts, game has returned to the area in healthy numbers and on some days one may even catch a glimpse of an elephant in the Omaruru riverbed!

Each year in September the Omaruru Artist's Trail attracts streams of visitors from all over the country, as local artists open their homes, studios and galleries, displaying their art (from sculptures and paintings to wood carvings and photography) and giving interactive craft demonstrations (including pottery and jewellery-making, basketweaving and marble sculpting) as well as allowing visitors a chance to sample local handmade chocolates and wine.

Amongst Omaruru's residents are two endemic bird species – the Rüppell's parrot and the Hartlaub's spurfowl (francolin) – as well as a small endemic carnivore – the black mongoose.

A centrepoint for life in Omaruru, Gudrun Mueller's popular Omaruru Souvenirs & Kaffeestube is housed in the century-old historical and handsome Wronsky House. Built as a general trading store by Wilhelm Wronsky after he settled in Omaruru from Berlin in the 1890s, many of the original tiles, ceiling wood and fittings still remain, all transported by boat from Germany and then by ox wagon from the coast.

Located at Nawa Nawa, Omaruru's popular arts and crafts complex, the Touch Goldsmith is renowned throughout the country and worldwide for its finely crafted jewellery. Owner and master goldsmith Anette Meyer emigrated from Germany to Namibia in 2002, bringing international expertise and the finest hand to the business today, creating pieces inspired by Namibia's landscapes.

Omuntu Garden

SCULPTURAL ART AND PEACE PARK

Laid out over 3 000 square metres, the serene, shady Omuntu Garden is filled with more than 50 sculptures – the largest space exhibiting sculptures permanently in Namibia. Sometimes striking, sometimes quirky but always thought provoking, each piece is made by a local artist in the garden.

Gallery owner, yoga teacher and artist extraordinaire, Hanne Marott-Alpers is the unofficial doyenne of the dynamic Omaruru art scene. Danish-born Hanne has been permanently residing in Omaruru since 2005, following a legal career in the United Kingdom where she had a Masters in Law and BA in Political Science and East Asian Cultures. Hanne is self-taught in creative scrap compositions, water colour and ink washes, and her creative work and inquiring mind continue to inspire all who meet her and those who visit her renowned Omuntu Garden which she curates.

The aim of Omuntu Garden is to nurture and support local talent, opening up opportunities for aspiring artists by providing them with tools and space to develop their art, resulting in powerful works by artists such as Alfeus Mvula, Seth Forthmeyer, Samwele Kamati, Paulo Cachinga and Abniel Enkali.

In 2013 Hanne created a monumental art installation as part of the nationwide multi-artist collaboration 'Land Matters in Art', an initiative under the auspices of the Minister of Lands and Resettlement, designed to tackle controversial land issues. Hanne's 'Is Our Water Safe In Your Hands?' installation and 'happening' consisted of 5 000 reeds topped with fluttering blue flags. Placed in the shape of a spiral in the middle of the dry Omaruru riverbed and covering approximately 9 240 square metres, the bold 330 metre-long, 28 metre-wide installation gives an impression of the river in flow. Amongst the reeds an oversized shark's fin ominously symbolises the 'shark' mentality of senseless water consumption, and foreboding bleached animal bones lay scattered at the end of the surreal river to show the effects on the land if the water runs out.

The stirring and ambitious project involved over 30 volunteers from the Omaruru community and beyond: from school children to pensioners and native Namibians to German tourists.

The garden, on 53 Willhelm Zeraua Road, is open to the public on Saturdays or by appointment.

Camp Mara

ERONGO MOUNTAINS

Characterised by colourful landscapes, ancient rock art and spectacular geological phenomena, the Erongo region is one of Namibia's most diverse environments. The region contains, and is named after, the mighty Mount Erongo – a mountain rising to 2 319 metres and stretching 40 kilometres in diameter. It is the largest of the late-Mesozoic alkaline complexes of central-west Namibia.

Situated some 13 kilometres from the town of Omaruru, at the edge of the granite outcrops of the Erongo Mountains, is the intimate Camp Mara – blending in seamlessly with its surroundings, guests are introduced to the distinctive experience of Erongo wilderness tranquility.

The remarkable biodiversity in the area is a result of a rare convergence of ecosystems – from the arid Namib Desert approaching from the west to the eastern lush mixed-woodland savannah. The area is filled with an abundance of wildlife, including leopard, brown hyaena, mountain zebra, kudu, oryx, springbok, klipspringer and Damara dik-dik.

Camp Mara is located in the heart of the region and perfectly situated to explore its many facets. Charismatic owner Eckhard Meyer organises drive tour adventures through Namibia (and up to the Victoria Falls), including dry riverbed expeditions in search of the rare desert elephant.

Most notably, the Erongo region is a renowned hotspot of endemic and near-endemic plant, reptile, bird and mammal species, including the rock python, lovebird, and Hartmann's zebra.

Herero

Namibia's Herero are a pastoral, cattle-breeding people who migrated to Namibia several centuries ago, and form an integral part of the country's history. Folklore recollects a country known as Roruru, where the Herero originally lived a nomadic existence herding their cattle from one watering place to another, although no one has succeeded in tracing this legendary marshland. Legend has it that the Herero moved southwards from Roruru, arriving at the Kunene River in the 1500s. Some 200 years of Herero life in Kaokoland (now the Kunene Region) has been well documented and while the Himba and Tjimba tribes of the Herero group remained there, a large splinter group moved further south towards the central areas of Namibia around Omaruru, Okahandja, Otjimbingwe, the Waterberg and further east, where they adopted a more settled pastoralism with permanent abodes.

The story of the Herero is marred with tragedy and their survival has been hard-won. The early nineteenth century brought frequent cattle raids on the Herero by Topnaar and Orlam tribes, and between 1904 and 1907 the Herero faced a horrific genocide during the Herero German War, when General Lothar von Trotha introduced his infamous *Vernichtungsbefehl* (proclamation of extermination) – a foreboding precursor to the Second World War atrocities of Nazi Germany. An estimated 80 per cent of the Herero population perished during this first genocide of the twentieth century.

Each year on Maharero Day, the annual Herero Festival in the streets of Okahandja is a reminder of the incredible resilience of the Herero people who today, with over 130 000 Herero-speaking Namibians, remain a proud people with tribal solidarity and traditions intact.

The Herero have a bilateral descent system – the paternal line (*oruzo*) dictates a person's status in the family hierarchy, the place of abode, and traditions, while the maternal line (*eanda*) guides control and inheritance of moveable wealth.

The unique traditional Herero dress is a distinctive sight throughout the country. Influenced by the wives of missionaries in the nineteenth century, the colourful dress, known to the Herero as *ohorokweva*, is seemingly incongruous with the hot climate of the country. Resembling a colonial Victorian style with a bold-patterned, brightly coloured twist, *ohorokweva* may contain as much as 12 metres of fabric and are voluminously worn over several layers of petticoats. A Herero woman is not fully dressed unless she wears the *otjikaeva* headdress – its two pointed ends symbolising cattle horns. Common accessories include strings of sweet-smelling wooden beads carved from tamboti wood, known as *otupapa*, as well as modern jewellery such as rings, bangles and brooches.

Etusis Lodge

KARIBIB, DAMARALAND
(NOW KNOWN AS THE KUNENE REGION)

Set amongst contrasting landscapes that vary between gently undulating savannah, white marble hills and the Otjipatera mountain range that rises up to nearly 2 000 metres, is the remarkable Etusis Lodge, harmoniously blending into the environment of the Etusis Nature Reserve covering more than 21 000 hectares and approximately 1 200 metres above sea level.

The nature reserve is filled with an abundance of wildlife and a diverse range of species, including cheetah, leopard, African wild cat, Cape fox, brown hyaena and over 100 different kinds of birds. Most notable in the area are the Hartmann's mountain zebra, as the lodge is home to the renowned Etusis Foundation, a non-profit organisation established to conserve the highly-endangered species. The foundation was created following extensive research into the territories, densities and migrations of the Hartmann's mountain zebra within the Etusis Game Reserve by passionate conservationist Volker Ledermann (co-founder of edding AG, proprietary eponym and renowned manufacturer of felt-tip pens and permanent markers). Today Namibia is home to the largest population of Hartmann's mountain zebra, yet they live in direct conflict with local farmers due to the fact that they are in direct competition regarding livestock grass and fodder – an increasingly scarce commodity in many parts of the country.

The ever-increasing list of activities at Etusis includes game drives (by 4x4 or eco-friendly horse-drawn carriage), horse riding, mountain biking, telescope stargazing, kite flying, mineral sample collecting, marked nature hikes and rock climbing amongst the unique geology of the Otjipatera Mountains.

The area surrounding Etusis Lodge is one of the world's great geological marvels. In the ancient Abbabis Complex visitors can observe one of the oldest rock formations of Namibia, which already existed some 2 000 million years ago when life was only possible in the form of micro-organisms. Here one can stand on the deepest roots of the African continent.

Dawn breaks on the ancient and majestic Spitzkoppe, an imposing granite formation situated 60 kilometres north-west of Usakos en route to Swakopmund. The sharply pointed Groot (large) Spitzkoppe, sometimes referred to as 'The Matterhorn of Africa', rises 600 metres above the Namib Desert plains and is believed to be over 700 million years old.

The Spitzkoppe are the upper part of a giant batholith, an enormous piece of granite moving from deep within the earth's mantle towards the surface. Far underground, the lower part of the Spitzkoppe is still magma, while the upper regions have solidified very slowly into granite. A climbing and camping favourite, the Spitzkoppe peak was first ascended in 1946.

SWAKOPMUND

A place of magic, where the icy ocean meets a mighty sea of dunes

Between the icy-cold Atlantic Ocean and the sea of torrid Namib Desert dunes lies the coastal town of Swakopmund, its wide streets lined with palm trees, brightly coloured flowerbeds and old-world German colonial architecture. Namibia's premier seaside resort, 280 kilometres west of Windhoek, has a unique atmosphere, seemingly out of place and time, and attracts visitors and locals en-masse with its kindly cooler climate, especially during the searing summer months.

When Walvis Bay was in British hands, Germany needed an alternative harbour to gain access to the interior of the land it had colonised. The task to find a suitable site fell to Captain Curt von François and the crew of the *Hyäne* ('Hyaena'), and in August 1892 their search ended near the mouth of the Swakop River, where they erected two beacons on the shore to mark the landing site. The site didn't offer natural protection to ships lying off the coast, but its attraction lay in the valuable availability of fresh water. Not long after the initial 120 Schutztruppe soldiers and 40 settlers arrived on shore, Swakopmund became a busy main port for imports and exports, and received municipal status in 1909.

Swakopmund (German for 'Mouth of the Swakop') was officially given its name in 1886, succeeding the original name Swachaub given by the first settlers, and perhaps a little kinder than the original Herero name for the area, Otjozondjii derived from the Nama word *Tsoakhaub* ('excrement opening'), describing the Swakop River in flood carrying debris to the Atlantic Ocean, often including dead animals. Today, locals affectionately call their town Swakop.

Several unsuccessful attempts to create an artificial harbour (including the construction a 375-metre pier, which was quickly blocked up by a consequential sandbank, courtesy of the northward sweeping Benguela Current) resulted in Swakopmund's main beach area, known as the The Mole. Today The Mole and the adjacent Palm Beach provide a favourite, although icy, swimming area and The Mole's lee is popularly used as a mooring for yachts.

Like its seemingly incongruous location between wild sea and silent desert, Swakopmund can somehow be experienced as both a bustling, energetic and modern town and a laid-back, quaint hamlet of a bygone era. The distinct German feel is unmistakable – the colonial architecture very much sets the town's feel, and this continues in the wide selection of authentic German restaurants, delicatessens, master bakeries and traditional German-beer-serving Brauhäuser.

Street names, too, carry on the German tradition, with examples including Bismarck, Schlachter and Dr Schwietering streets that still exist today. After Namibian independence in 1990, however, many street names were changed from their original colonial-era German names, to honor Namibians: Kaiser-Wilhelm-Straße became Sam Nujoma Avenue, Brücken Street was changed to Albertina Amathila and Bahnhof Street is now known as Theo-Ben Gurirab Avenue. A fitting mix for the town's strong German and Namibian direction!

Swakopmund is highly regarded for its trade in authentic Namibian products, both traditional and modern. Renowned handcrafted leather work is available, as is a wide selection of distinctly Namibian art and crafts. One can also find Namibian textiles, handmade jewellery, semiprecious stones, ostrich eggshell beads and even Himba metal beads and ornate Owambo *ekipa* buttons. Swakopmund is also home to the world's largest quartz crystal cluster (weighing over 14 000 kilograms and believed to be 520 million years old), which is on display at the museum/shop Kristall Galerie.

Swakopmund's popular state-of-the-art National Marine Aquarium, located on the beachfront, underwent an extensive upgrade in 2012 and provides visitors with an enthralling introduction to the icy Benguela Current's aquatic life. With 17 tanks, a large 12 x 8-metre oval-shaped walk-through tunnel and touch pools (including an interactive experience with stingrays), tourists have ample opportunity to observe spotted shark, sand shark, kabeljou, steenbras and galjoen to name a few.

At the foot of Swakopmund's lighthouse is the fascinating Swakopmund Museum, arguably the most thought-provoking and educational of any in Namibia. The museum, which was founded by Dr Alfons Weber in 1951, occupies the site of the old harbour warehouse, which was destroyed in 1914 by a 'lucky' shot from a British warship. Although small, the museum is jam-packed with fascinating displays showcasing local natural history, mineralogy, botany as well as an overview of the diverse and distinct population groups of Namibia. Visitors are also provided a glimpse into early Swakopmund life with a reconstructed colonial home interior, Emil Kiewittand's apothecary shop, uniforms of the Camel Corps and 'Shell furniture' (so called because it was homemade from 1930s depression-era petrol and paraffin tins). Amongst the many interesting pieces are meteorite chunks, shipwreck finds, jawbones of our human ancestors and restored ox-wagons and turn-of-the-century drawing rooms. The museum also houses the Rössing Room, an exhibit that depicts the uranium mining process. A regular tour from the museum takes visitors to the actual Rössing mine, located some 55 kilometres east of Swakopmund, which is the largest open-pit uranium mine in the world and has the capacity to produce some 5 000 short tons of uranium oxide per year.

Colonial Architecture & Ludwig Schröder

Swakopmund's inimitable style and charm is undoubtedly in its architecture – first seen as a curious mirage of domes, steeples, turrets and towers as one approaches from the interior. Streets are lined with unmistakably German-style colonial architecture, beautifully preserved and on an awe-inspiring scale. Many of the buildings date back to the early 1900s, having been built shortly after the first German settlers arrived. Although one can't help imagining a grand *Jugendstil* party behind each façade, today many of these well-maintained masterpieces house shops, offices and more increasingly residential apartments and private homes.

Unsurprisingly the Swakopmund property market continues to grow apace each year, as demand increases and suitable land on this precarious coastline becomes scarcer. Visitors to Swakopmund are invariably charmed by the architecture and the laid-back, yet sophisticated local scene, while potential investors soon become aware of the immense popularity of this small coastal town, especially during the late months of the year when temperatures become unbearable for many in the country's interior.

Ludwig Schröder House, a stately structure built in 1913, originally served as the premises of the *Südwestafrikanische Boden-Kredit-Gesellschaft*, the colony's first credit institution. A tenant of the building, and subsequently its owner from 1949, was Ludwig Schröder, after whom the building is now known. One of early Swakopmund's best known personalities, Ludwig Schröder was a German immigrant who served as Mayor of Swakopmund and vice-chairperson of the Chamber of Commerce. The Schröder family are still very much a presence in Swakopmund, today serving the town as the area's leading estate agent – and undoubtedly the most knowledgeable having been established in 1919!

Perhaps the finest architectural example is the magnificent Hohenzollern Building (*this page left*) – an elegant three-storey building constructed between 1905 and 1906 as a hotel. Designed in the Victorian baroque tradition, the building is adorned with decorative relief. Perched at the top of the corner entrance is a large sculpture of Atlas holding up the world. For fear of it tumbling down, the original stucco figure was replaced with a lighter fibreglass replica in the 1980s.

22° South

In 1902, situated at the end of the Mole, a humble beacon was erected, soon to be washed away by the powerful South Atlantic rollers. A year later an 11-metre-high lighthouse was built on the 11-metre-high dune that overlooked the Mole Basin, its light helping to guide ships as far as 14 nautical miles away. In 1910, following a dramatic increase in traffic to the port of Swakopmund, the structure was raised another 10 metres, enabling the light to be seen for 35 nautical miles. Today, Swakopmund's iconic lighthouse stands sentinel over the shoreline, a proud and prominent landmark of the coastal city.

Situated in and around its base is one of Swakopmund's most popular restaurants, 22° South. The unique location, whether dining inside the cosy candle-lit rooms or eating alfresco between the bold red-and-white striped landmark and the rising palm trees of the city's coast, provides an unrivalled dreamy setting, blending history, maritime romance and the city's finest authentic Italian cuisine.

Ever-present owners and husband-and-wife team Esbi and Silvio add their unique international flair to the restaurant's old-world charm and the Mediterranean cuisine is inspired – from fresh pasta, crispy-base pizzas and homemade gelato to an extensive variety of seafood that is as fresh as one would expect from a restaurant only moments from the water's edge.

Art Africa

African art dates back thousands of years and has always been a powerful unifying voice of a continent filled with myriad tribes, cultures and traditions. From the ancient San rock art (examples of which date back some 28 000 years) to the ubiquitous heavily stylised traditional masks; from powerful figurative sculpture to intricate jewellery made from diverse materials such as tiger's eye stone, haematite, sisal, coconut shell, beads and ebony wood, the art of the continent continues to inspire all who encounter it.

Although mistaken as 'primitive' by the western world, its sheer power and complexity was 'rediscovered' in the early twentieth century by artists such as Picasso, Matisse and Vincent van Gogh who saw within it a formal perfection and sophistication unified with phenomenal expressive power. This influenced the primarily aesthetic function of western art to an expression of imagination, emotion and mystical and religious experience – all that was present in African art since the dawn of time.

Art Africa, on Swakopmund's Tobias Hainyeko Street, was founded in 1999 by the passionate and knowledgeable Bubble Burns and today is the epicentre for local art in the coastal town. It is jam-packed with tribal art, artifacts, crafts, and locally-inspired jewellery, clothing and décor. Its lush garden setting is home to the ever-popular alfresco Garden Café, which leads to the newly launched fashion boutique, *EARTH*. Adjacent to the main Art Africa shop is an authentic alleyway outdoor crafts market, where local artists are given a space to personally exhibit their paintings and crafts seven days a week, giving visitors the chance to meet the artists and watch them produce their work.

Bojos Café

With its European flair and laid-back coastal lifestyle it's no surprise that Swakopmund has a buzzing coffee culture. Coffee connoisseurs are spoilt for choice with close to 30 coffee shops throughout the town, providing that all-important caffeine fix. But perhaps the best known and most loved of them all, by both locals and tourists alike, is the ever-popular Bojos Café. Situated in the timelessly classical Hansa Hotel building (dating back to 1905) Bojos Café has been *the* place to go since it first opened its doors in 1996.

Quirky and fun, Bojo Café's décor is an extension of owners Kelly Hicks and Bobby Jo Bassingthwaighte's personalities. The walls are filled with photographs, cartoons, memorabilia and sayings, some about coffee ('Everyone should believe in something, I believe I'll have another coffee!') and some with off-centre wisdom on life ('Life is tough, get a helmet'), as well as a feast of murals and musings by celebrated local artist Nadine Downing.

Of course, it all boils down to the coffee and in this regard Bojos Café is in a league of its own. Through an introduction by a satiated and appreciative Australian tourist, Kelly and Bobby Jo enlisted the help of Five Senses Coffee's Dean Gallagher, one of the world's leading authorities on the subject. Dean travelled to Namibia to assist the Bojos team in the fine art of freshly roasted coffee making and the results are evident in the café's devoted following of regulars.

To complement the coffee Kelly prepares sumptuous food and freshly baked treats daily (including the author's favourite chocolate fudge brownies) and is adamant about using local, fresh and organic ingredients. Equally high on Bojos' agenda is recycling, and Kelly and Bobby Jo do all they can to promote eco-friendliness and avoid wastage. Discarded food and coffee grounds are used for compost at the staff's living grounds and Kelly is a proactive educator of communities, most notably inspiring a strong recycling culture in the nearby town of Wlotzkasbaken.

Swakopmund's Guesthouses

With Swakopmund being one of the country's most popular holiday destinations, the seaside town is brimming with accommodation choices – from budget-friendly backpackers to luxurious opulence. Swakopmund guesthouses are renowned, not only for their high international standards, but also for their unique, charming and creative offerings.

Cornerstone Guesthouse (*top right*) with its luscious garden is a small family-run bed and breakfast in Swakopmund's 'old town', lovingly created and managed by owners Peter and Margo Bassingthwaighte. Peter, a sixth-generation Namibian is a descendant of the country's oldest English-speaking pioneer settler family. In 1844 Frank Bassingthwaighte, an English blacksmith from Bristol, was en route to Australia when he was persuaded to land at Walvis Bay. His ensuing adventures in the vast, largely unmapped land of Namibia have become the stuff of legend.

Built high up on stilts on the edge of the dry Swakop riverbed, the wooden, thatched chalets of **The Stiltz** (*top left*) are linked together by walkways and offer a truly unique and breathtaking view of the Atlantic Ocean, the Swakop riverbed, the sand dunes and the bird-rich lagoon of the river mouth. The creative vision of well-known local architect Danie Holloway, The Stiltz provides an inimitable atmosphere of romance and sumptuous attention to detail.

Charming, cosy and family friendly, **Sandfields Guesthouse** (*bottom right*) reflects the warmth and creativity of its owners Jean and Richard Downing and Paul Liechti. The artist-filled Downing family is renowned in Namibia and Richard, an architect, lovingly created the guesthouse, filling it with exquisite wooden details including the pictured heirloom from his Swiss-German grandfather.

The award-winning self-catering bed and breakfast **Brigadoon** (*bottom left*) is one of Swakopmund's hidden accommodation gems – behind its suburban façade is a peaceful oasis brimming with birdlife in a lush palm-treed garden, where breakfasts are served on each room's private patio. Like Cornerstone's Peter, owner Bubbles is also from the Bassingthwaighte family and the name Brigadoon was also that of the Khomas region Bassingthwaighte farm.

Offering guests an African experience with a European touch, Organic Square Guesthouse, located close to the centre of town, is the creative vision of chic Swakopmund local Heidi Kriess. With an organic approach to design, Heidi added her personal touch to an old house, converting it into a modern lime-green-infused oasis, where original elements have been 'up-cycled' with flair, such

as breakfast tables lovingly created from timeworn doors. Breakfast at the guesthouse's Zen Eatery is naturally organic too, with homemade fruit juices and home-baked bread, set in a garden with freshly-grown herbs and the perfect soundtrack – the sounds of the lapping waves of the Atlantic Ocean less than 500 metres away.

The Tug Restaurant

A tourist attraction in its own right, The legendary Tug restaurant is Swakopmund's most popular seafood eatery. Situated at the foot of the old iron pier, The Tug, as its name suggests, is in fact built around an old oil-fired tugboat – the *Danie Hugo*. Named after a South African railway commissioner from Dal Josafat, the *Danie Hugo* was launched in 1958 and remained in service for over 20 years before finally being broken up in 1984 in the Walvis Bay port.

Under the direction of local visionary architect Danie Holloway, the 812 gross ton tugboat was lovingly transformed into a delightfully unusual and authentic restaurant, and The Tug opened its doors in December 1993. Although no longer pulling ships, The Tug quickly began to pull in the crowds and on any given evening the restaurant buzzes with a bouillabaisse of cultures – tourists, locals, movie stars, politicians and, even on the rare occasion, royalty!

Inside, the atmospheric tug interior is filled with original tugboat elements, from hatches and handrails to traditional lifebuoys, and continuing the all-important seafaring tradition, a cozy memorabilia-filled bar is situated in the old officer's cabin quarters. For a more contemporary twist, many of the dining tables at The Tug restaurant have been adorned in various nautical themes painted by some of Namibia's best known artists, including John Randall, Joe Madisa, Jenny Gorman and Nadine Downing.

Unobstructed views of the coastline add to the romance and drama of The Tug and spray from the crashing waves of the cold Atlantic splash teasingly against the sizeable windows. Upstairs, on the tugboat's bridge, diners are surrounded by a 360-degree panoramic view of the shoreline, town and dunes, while the decked terrace is Swakopmund's ultimate spot for an end-of-day apéritif, surrounded by the sound of crashing waves and embraced by the salty sea air.

The flavoursome fresh local food served at The Tug has earned the restaurant a sterling reputation, particularly for their local Walvis Bay oysters, West Coast lobster and fresh Swakop River asparagus.

The Tug Restaurant's terrace overlooks Swakopmund's landmark jetty, which was originally built in 1905. After naval shipworm damage, construction of an iron jetty replacement began in 1911. It was declared a pedestrian walkway following the First World War.

Desert Breeze Lodge

Only a few minutes from the centre of town, the surrounding environment and view from Desert Breeze Lodge is nothing short of breathtaking. From its prime position above the ephemeral Swakop River, the luxurious lodge overlooks a vast and sensuous apricot-coloured dune sea. While other establishments famously boast endless sea views, as would be fitting of such a renowned coastal town, Desert Breeze offers a sea view of a different sandy nature – the ultimate desert experience from a most unlikely place.

The lodge is the latest creation of local visionary, designer and part-owner Danie Holloway, the same creative mind that crafted Swakopmund's other defining contemporary establishments – The Tug Restaurant and The Stiltz Bed & Breakfast, as well as The Raft in nearby Walvis Bay.

Here one can savour a desert view at its best – ever transforming at the whim of the prevailing south-west winds and deepening in hue at different times of the day. Unmistakable, as one enters the lodge, is the dreamlike view dramatically framed by the large glass panels of the central building, a view that can also be enjoyed from each of the 12 bungalows with private sun decks, or in incomparable luxury from the secluded three-roomed villa. The mesmerising, lively architecture stands proudly and brilliantly in bold shades of bright turquoise, lime green, topaz blue and burnt orange. The sharp levels, angles and lines of the architecture give the lodge a remarkable energy, and the use of materials is an endless feast for the eye – from recovered jetty-pole beams to authentic northern Namibian pestle-and-mortar flour-grinders, no corner of the lodge is left without thought.

In and amongst the chalets, with the grandeur of the red-hued dunes as their background, enchanting larger-than-life stone sculptures add raw energy and power to Swakopmund's oldest (and newest) view.

THE LIVING DESERT

Tommy Collard and the hidden fauna and flora of a not-so-barren desert

Although arid and seemingly inhospitable, the boundless dunes just south of Swakopmund are filled with rich and complex flora and fauna, all remarkably adapted over millions of years for desert survival.

In the 1990s local naturalist Tommy Collard developed 'The Living Desert Tour', taking locals and tourists through from the life-rich eastern side of the dunes to the Atlantic Ocean on the western side of the dune belt. Tommy's innate knack for skilfully tracking the shy, intriguing creatures of the desert and his infectious brand of enthusiasm has made the Living Desert Tour one of the most popular activities in the area.

Known locally as 'the bushman's newspaper', the abundance of micro-activity in and amongst the dunes can be 'read' each morning by the many tracks and markings on the sand. Here one can find fascinating creatures endemic to the Namib: caterpillar-like tracks on a dune slip face are the tell-tale sign of a nearby Peringuey's desert adder (also known as the sidewinding adder), a well-camouflaged snake that uses its unique, mesmerising sidewinding motion to move across the fluidic substrate quickly and with minimal contact with the hot sand. Its eyes are located on top of its short, flat head, an adaption for its ambush hunting technique, where it buries itself beneath the surface of the sand in patient anticipation of a lizard or gecko.

Equally fascinating is the delightful palmato gecko – a rainbow-coloured gecko with a beautiful transparent body endemic to the Namib – with its uniquely webbed feet that act like sand shoes in the dune sand. The palmato gecko uses a high-pitched squeaking sound to frighten attackers, and licks condensed fog off its large eyelidless, fixed-lens eyes as a source of water.

The Namaqua chameleon (*left*) is the only true desert dwelling chameleon on earth and is the fastest moving chameleon in the world – a full grown chameleon (which can measure 28.5 centimetres from its nose to tip of the tail) can cover 300 metres in 20 minutes. Two other notably speedy Namib creatures include the gecko *Rhoptropus afer*, the fastest gecko on the planet, and the beetle *Onymacris plana*, found south of Walvis Bay, which can move at a speed of three kilometres per hour over the hot Namib sands. The Namaqua chameleon's most famous adaptation is its ability to change colour – when on the move early morning or late afternoon, the side of its body facing the sun will be a heat-absorbing dark colour while its opposite side will be lighter to reflect the heat. The tongue of the Namaqua chameleon can reach the entire length of its body including the tail – a useful extension when catching beetles, crickets, scorpions and even baby chameleons, which it hunts in both the sandy dunes and rocky areas. Tommy and his team follow the Namaqua chameleon with keen interest, having microchip-tagged a number of them to provide fresh insight into their fascinating behaviour.

The endemic shovel-snouted lizard, also commonly known as the sand-diving lizard, can be found along dune slip faces where the sand is soft. If threatened, the lizard swiftly dives into the soft sand for protection, as well as to regulate body temperature. Its other name is the thermal dancing lizard – during the heat of the day the lizard can be seen 'dancing' by holding two of its feet in the air at a time, minimising the heat transferred from the sand to the body.

One of the most beguiling creatures endemic to the Namib is the dancing white lady spider (also known as the golden wheel spider). Prey to parasitic pompilid wasps, who hunt and paralyse spiders as food for their larvae, the dancing white lady spider, as its name hints, has a fascinating escape tactic. Diving off the dune's steep slip face, it flips on its side and cartwheels down the dune at an astonishing speed of 44 turns per second – faster than a wasp can fly. When it reaches the bottom, it stands with four legs in the air 'dancing' in defence should any other predators be present. Continuing its unusual practices, the dancing white lady spider does not produce a web. Instead it buries itself in a silk-lined burrow extending 40–50 centimetres deep, which it closes with a diminutive silk trap door. During the process of digging its burrow, the spider can shift up to 10 litres (or 80 000 times its body weight) of sand.

Survival for much of the desert's flora and fauna is dependent on the life-giving fog that consistently rolls in from the icy Atlantic Ocean. The endemic dollar bush with its fleshy coin-resembling leaves is found scattered in between the dunes, and the pencil bush is able to reverse transpiration by absorbing water through its leaves and transporting it down to its roots.

The fog-basking, head-standing beetle *Onymacris unquicularis*, a unique inhabitant of Namib coastal dunes, is able to survive by collecting water from early morning fog on its bumpy back. Standing on a small ridge of sand using its long, spindly legs, the beetle faces into the breeze with its body angled at 45 degrees and tiny droplets of moisture slide downwards towards its mouth. It can absorb 40 per cent of its entire body mass in one morning.

In the late afternoon on the side of the dunes the wind and sand join in a playful interaction – fanning out, whirling, skipping and all of a sudden gathering before spinning like a miniature twister, then abruptly fanning out and settling in the doldrums of peace and still silence as if taking a breather…just to be scooped up and launched into the next play…'Sand ballet!' as Tommy so aptly puts it.

YEEHAA! @ Swakopmund

Although a coastal town, Swakopmund is by no means sleepy. Dubbed 'Namibia's Adventure Capital', Swakopmund offers thrill-seeking locals and tourists a wide array of adventure activities to suit every whim.

QUAD BIKING

Swakopmund's most popular action adventure is undoubtedly quad biking through the rolling expanse of shifting dunes that surround the town. Every year thousands of adventurers take up the challenge with Desert Explorers, the leading quad bike operator in the country, zipping, zooming and revving their way through the Swakop riverbed into the dune belt. Those wanting a more relaxed pace get a chance to experience pristine beauty of the Namib desert in areas inaccessible by 4x4 vehicles and those pursuing action get the chance to blast through berms, spirals and slopes via the Roller Coasters to the top of Big Billy and down the Devil's Dip towards the Table Top, an imposing dune offering a spectacular view of the mighty Atlantic.

SANDBOARDING

Sandboarding on Swakopmund's surrounding dunes has become increasingly popular for the ultimate heart-pumping adrenaline rush. The first professional sandboarding operation on the Namibian coast, Alter-Action was founded in 1996 by Chris Jason and Beth Sarro and today remains the go-to company for sandboarding excursions, offering the safest and most effective method of sliding on the dunes. First-timers and seasoned boarders are taken to Alter-Action's 'perfect' dune – a star dune with six different faces and a towering height of 100 metres, just over 10 kilometres from Swakopmund. Alter-Action's speediest ride, complete with extra layers of sandboard polish and gallantry, is known as the infamous Dizzy – an experience allowing sandboarders the rush of reaching speeds of 80 kilometres per hour!

SKYDIVING

Seven days a week, 365 days a year, Swakopmund's Ground Rush Adventures gives brave souls the unforgettable thrill of their life as they take to the skies over one of the most spectacular drop zones on earth – the sprawling Namib Desert, adjacent to the expansive Atlantic Ocean. Whether tandem skydiving, accelerated freefalling or static line jumping, soaring through Namibia's pristine air with a view over an ancient geological wonderland is truly indescribable. As testament to the thrill, owners Matthias Röttcher and Craig Milne, who opened Ground Rush Adventures in 1997, have personally skydived over 7 000 and 10 000 times respectively (and respectfully).

Okakambe Trails

Situated at the edge of the Namib Desert on the outskirts of Swakopmund, Okakambe Trails is the culmination of German horse riding enthusiast Kathrin Schaefer Stiege's dream to open a horse riding school amidst the vast landscapes of Africa. Today the small horse farm hosts over 38 healthy, well-trained horses, including Hanoverians, Thoroughbreds, Arabs and Fresians. Okakambe means 'horse' in the native Herero and Oshivambo languages and the horse-back adventures on offer are simply breathtaking, making Okakambe Trails hugely popular amongst local and visiting horse enthusiasts from all over the world and all walks of life.

For adventurers and experienced riders there are overnight trails from one day, two days and up to seven days, offering the incomparable trailblazing experience of freedom that Namibia's vast pristine landscapes offer. Pony rides are available for children and there are also popular hourly tourist out-rides, which take riders into the Namib Desert, with its variety of canyons and plains. The trails lead through the dry Swakop riverbed, amongst unique fauna and flora, past small water pools and into the silence of the dramatic moon-like landscape. Here one can enjoy the vastness of the oldest desert in the world on a sunset ride, being in touch with nature through the movement of the horse or watching the full moon rise whilst riding after dark on a 'moonshine' excursion.

Abenteuer Afrika Safari

MOON VALLEY

Namibia's leading destination management company, Abenteuer Afrika Safari, was founded by Hilmar Tonnemacher and Dianne Orban in 1993, pioneering incentive travel in the country and offering experiences simply unrivalled on the continent.

Imagine the scene – a large group of executives end an eventful day of adventurous pursuits with sundowners in an unrevealed location. The sun is setting and the group are whisked through a winding route into the majestic geological theatre of the Moon Landscape. A final turn reveals an opening amidst the towering boulders where tables are set for fine dining and hundreds of candles flicker amidst the surrounding rocks. Oohs and aahs are silenced when the host announces that he forgot to bring the Champagne. 'Not to worry,' says the crowd in unison, the sheer magic of the environment being enough entertainment. Just then, an aeroplane buzzes overhead and tuxedo-clad skydivers leap from the craft, expertly landing moments later amongst the crowd, chilled Champagne bottles in hand!

This is a mere moment amongst many conceptualised and skillfully orchestrated by the Abenteuer Afrika Safari team – a culmination of exhaustive product knowledge, years of experience, a country filled with incomparable natural venues and a company focused on its motto: 'creative minds playing at work'.

Hilmar and Dianne had the enterprising notion of offering their guests guided tours of the Moon Landscape – a natural phenomena 30 kilometres east of Swakopmund, where the vast landscape, as its name suggests, appears eerily like the surface of the moon. Once a large mountain range pushed up through the earth's surface over 500 million years ago, the lunar landscape was carved by the Swakop River and its many tributaries as it flowed through the valley for some two million years.

Today, Abenteuer Afrika Safari offers a wide range of services from special events to conferences to luxury private travel and their enviable track record includes high-profile clients such as Angelina Jolie and Brad Pitt, and legendary African explorer Kingsley Holgate.

The bustling harbour city of Walvis Bay, some 30 kilometres south of Swakopmund, lies just north of the Tropic of Capricorn in the Kuiseb River delta. The only natural harbour of any size along the country's coast, its natural deepwater harbour, protected by the Pelican Point sand spit, is a haven for sea vessels and a hub for Namibia's renowned fishing industry. The much-colonised bay has

witnessed a colourful and complex political history given its unique location in relation to the sea route around the Cape of Good Hope. Despite the fact that Walvis Bay has an arid climate – it receives less than 10 millimetres of precipitation per year, making it one of the driest cities on the planet – temperatures are curiously mild due to cold offshore currents.

Sandwich Harbour 4x4

The giant dune scapes and pristine lagoon of Sandwich Harbour lie some 55 kilometres south of Walvis Bay. Famed for its abundant birdlife and breathtaking scenery, this is an area often read about but rarely visited, making it an idyllic section of the Namib-Naukluft Park to experience the rare silent isolation so characteristic of Sandwich Harbour and the Skeleton Coast.

The *Sandwich*, after which the area is named, was the first recorded ship to have set anchor in the vicinity in the early 1790s. Its curious name may well have been a corruption of the German word *Sandfisch* (the name of a shark type found in the surrounding waters). Sporadic activity followed throughout the years – when the British took control of Walvis Bay, German ships utilised Sandwich Harbour as their port and in the 1930s there was a flurry of activity as an ambitious project began to build a guano island in the lagoon using sand pumps imported from Holland. Unfortunately hopes of capitalising on the valuable natural fertiliser were dashed when it was discovered that jackals could cross to the island at low tides, chasing the birds (and investors) away. Poor infrastructure and unstable accessibility eventually resulted in the harbour's abandonment and today little evidence is left of man's activities in the area.

There are no official roads leading to Sandwich Harbour and existing tracks quickly disappear due to the tides and strong winds. This as well as the large dunes, some rising over 100 metres, make the area challenging to access by most, however in 2009 Naude and Katja Dreyer launched Sandwich Harbour 4x4, offering visitors thrilling excursions to the heart of Sandwich Harbour and a chance to experience the magnificent area from dune-top lookouts to the water's edge.

The Sandwich Harbour lagoon is one of the country's finest birding spots. Declared a Ramsar site in 1995 and classified as Wetlands of International Importance, the area hosts more than 70 000 birds, many of which are seasonal migrants travelling from the northern hemisphere. Sandwich Harbour is also home to springbok, ostrich and the elusive brown hyaena, as well as black-backed jackal that have adeptly learnt to dig holes to access shallow ground-level water.

One of several shipwrecks visible today along the notoriously treacherous Skeleton Coast, *The Zeila* was stranded in the early morning hours on 25 August 2008. The fishing trawler was heading for Mumbai, India, when it came loose from its towing line and met its fate near 'Die Walle', a popular fishing spot approximately 55 kilometres north of Swakopmund and 14 kilometres south of Henties Bay.

Wlotzkasbaken, 30 kilometres north of Swakopmund, is a surreal settlement of little more than 100 owner-built, unconventional and often eccentric homes and less than 10 permanent residents. The houses are all self-sustaining as Wlotzkasbaken is not electrified or connected to the public water system. Water is delivered by road and stored in private water towers, which characterise the settlement's unmistakable skyline.

Henties Bay

The coastal city of Henties Bay lies 70 kilometres north of Swakopmund. Although considerably smaller than its famous neighbour, the 121 square-kilometre Henties Bay has a population of approximately 3 300 and is a well-loved holiday spot. Each year thousands of fishing enthusiasts flock to the shore of Henties Bay for its renowned shark and rock and surf angling.

The town's namesake, Major Hendrik 'Henty' Stefanus van der Merwe, a Kalkfeld farmer, motor-dealer and big-game hunter, came across the area in 1929 while looking for water after an arduous hunting expedition. Long before, in 1488, after discovering an abundance of fish, Portuguese explorer Bartolomeu Dias named the coastline Praai das Sadhinas (Coast of Fish). The fresh water source was first discovered by the German Schutztruppe soldiers in 1886 and, in 1920, a minerals prospector who stayed for the night claimed that after tasting the coastal water he was healed from an affliction.

Passing through the town one is presented with an unexpected sight – the Henties Bay Golf Village (*right*). The unusual, sandy golf course is laid out in an old bed of the Omaruru River delta known as The Valley. With par 3, 4 and 5 holes, the nine-hole golf course extends over a distance of 2.7 kilometres and has well tended grass greens amongst its virgin desert sand fairways.

Outside of opening hours, one might catch a glimpse of Aaron Xoagub (*pictured right*), a local homeless teenager who regularly practices his swing using a discarded golf club found nearby. With only a single golf ball for practice, Aaron's improving game is an inspiration and adds new meaning to the 'game of patience'.

CAPE CROSS SEAL RESERVE

The Skeleton Coast's Cape fur seals and wild west coast waters

With tempestuous seas, a rugged coastline and a cacophony of bleats and barks, the Cape Cross Seal Reserve is home to the largest breeding colony of Cape fur seals on the planet.

Situated 53 kilometres north of the Atlantic coastal fishing town of Henties Bay and 120 kilometres north of Swakopmund, the small western Namibian headland along the Skeleton Coast, together with a surrounding area of 60 square kilometres consisting of flat gravel plains and a rocky outcrop, was proclaimed in 1968 to protect the biggest and best known of the 23 colonies of Cape fur seals that breed along the coast of South Africa and Namibia.

At Cape Cross the seal population fluctuates between an estimated 80 000 and 260 000. Visitors to the reserve can observe the cavorting gentle giants in their natural habitat from a 200-metre walkway constructed of recycled plastic. The non-stop action of thousands of Cape fur seals diving, basking, barking, squabbling, shuffling and waddling is a visual feast and a never-ending opportunity for photography, however the undeniable malodour can become equally overwhelming for some!

Cape fur seals (also known as brown fur seals) are endemic to the coastlines of southern Africa. The largest and most robust of fur seals, they are equally at home in the water and on land, and unlike 'true' seals they have a thick pelt (after which they are named) and external ear flaps, which give them their distinctive look.

The adult male Cape fur seal is just over two metres long and has a mass of 200–300 kilograms. Females are much smaller at 1.5 metres and weigh between 50 and 75 kilograms. Unsurprisingly the adult Cape fur seal has a healthy appetite and consumes about 270 kilograms of food each year – its diet consisting mainly of pilchards, Cape horse mackerel and rock lobster. They can dive as deep as 204 metres in search of food and can stay underwater for as long as 7.5 minutes. At sea the Cape fur seal's main predator is the great white shark and on land they are preyed upon by black-backed jackals and brown hyaenas. A number of antipredator strategies are employed by seals when in the water: swimming in large groups provides safety in numbers and low porpoising increases subsurface vigilance. When under the threat of attack the Cape fur seal darts in different directions to create confusion and swims as close as possible to the shark's dorsal fin, staying out of reach of the predator's jaws.

Each year, in mid-October, bulls come ashore to establish breeding colonies. A flurry of macho territorial fighting takes place, with much pushing, biting, barking and chest-to-chest combat, all of which can cause males to lose up to half of their body weight. Once a year, females breed in synchrony and after an eight-month gestation period give birth to a single pup. With tens of thousands of pups being born in a close time frame and proximity it's vital that the mother-infant recognition is strong. Suckling begins shortly after birth and the young pup's scent and sound plays an important identifying role. Survival for young seals is challenging, with prowling jackals and brown hyaenas never far away, and the infant mortality rate is approximately 30 per cent.

In 1484 Portuguese King João II ordered navigator and explorer Diogo Cão to advance south into undiscovered regions along the west coast of Africa. His first voyage took him south-west of today's Benguela, Angola and it was on his second voyage that he managed to reach almost 1 400 kilometres further, landing at the area known today as Cape Cross in January 1486. As the first European to set foot on Namibian soil, he proudly erected a *padrão* (limestone cross), after which Cape Cross gets its name.

In 1893, Diogo Cão's *padrão* was removed by German Navy captain Gottlieb Becker, commander of the SMS *Falke*, and taken to Cameroon where it was transferred to the steamship *Stettin* and taken to Wilhelmshaven in Germany. After several further transfers it made its way to the German Museum for Technology in Berlin.

Shortly after being removed from its original location, a simple wooden replica was erected in its place and around a century later a second replica was erected, this time more closely resembling the original. A translation of the *padrão's* inscription reads: '*In the year 6685 after the creation of the world and 1485 after the birth of Christ, the brilliant, far-sighted King John II of Portugal ordered Diogo Cão, knight of his court, to discover this land and to erect this padrão here*'.

In 1884 the first sightings of Cape fur seals were recorded off the coast of southern Africa, validated by entries in the log book of the German cruise ship, the *Möwe*.

Cape Cross Lodge

SKELETON COAST

Set on the edge of the bountiful Atlantic Ocean, along the coastline of the vast untamed, seldom-explored wilderness of the Skeleton Coast, is the luxurious Cape Cross Lodge, its architecture a mix of Cape Dutch and west coast fishing village charm.

Cape Cross Lodge is the only privately owned land on this coastline with a beachfront, making it unrivalled in its location for exploring the many captivating attributes of the area, whether your interest is geology, history, desert flora and fauna, photography, fishing, surfing, kayaking or simply relaxing.

Notably, the lodge is a mere four kilometres from the renowned Cape fur seal colony – the largest of its kind on the world, allowing guests to self-drive or even walk to the colony's wooden viewing deck amongst the rocky outcropped playground of thousands of Cape fur seals. Mercifully, guests are spared the characteristic odour of the colony as the hotel lies in a north-facing bay! Opportunistic black-backed jackals frequently prowl the edge of the colony, as do lurking brown hyaenas, although the latter prefer to do so under the cover of darkness.

Excursions from the lodge into the surrounding isolated mountainous area reveal the most fascinating phenomena of the region – from the prehistoric Messum Crater to ancient rock paintings, from Namibia's own 'dead sea' to a 400 year old petrified salt lagoon.

Here one finds the richest lichen stretches of the Namib Desert. The fog drifting in from the cold Atlantic provides the vital life-giving moisture for the organisms' survival. A symbiotic relationship between fungus and algae, lichens are found here in abundance and densely cover large areas, clinging to shrubs, rocks and pebbles of the gravel plains, many rare and endemic to the area.

A profusion of Namibia's iconic 'living fossil' *Welwitschia mirabilis* plants can be seen along the branches of the Messum River, some believed to be between 1 000 and 1 500 years old. The area is also home to the single largest specimen that exists today. Nicknamed 'The Big Welwitschia' the extraordinary plant stands 1.4 metres tall and is over four metres in diameter.

The Skeleton Coast

As a travel photographer and having experienced many of the world's great landscapes and attractions, I am often asked which is my favourite of all. Each time my answer is the same – 'Namibia from the air'. A visit to Swakopmund is not complete without a stop at the Scenic Air offices on Sam Nujoma Avenue to book a flight to spend an hour or two in a high-winged Cessna, soaring through the pristine air over the Sossusvlei dunes and along the formidable, desolate Skeleton Coast.

A bird's-eye view of Namibia gives an entirely new perspective on the country, and it is only from high up in the air that one truly appreciates the sheer vastness and raw power of the 'land of a thousand dunes'. Here one sees places so remote that it is unlikely to ever have been witnessed on foot by man; places so unharmed by pollution and modern development that one can only marvel at the vast landscapes and geological phenomena that almost certainly looked just like this in prehistoric times.

Namibia's famous and infamous Skeleton Coast National Park stretches from the Kunene River in the north to the Ugab River in the south, covering a massive total area of 16 000 square kilometres. Here the powerful endless ocean of the cold Atlantic abruptly encounters the powerful endless sea of sand, the sight of which is nothing short of astonishing. Tellingly, Namibia's San call the region 'The Land God Made in Anger', while Portuguese sailors would refer to it as 'The Gates of Hell'. The Skeleton Coast's name refers to the whale and seal bones that used to litter the shore from a once-bustling whaling industry, although the skeletons that characteristically remain today are those of shipwrecks, having met their fate by offshore rocks and fog along the treacherous coast. More than a thousand such vessels of various sizes litter the coast, notably the *Dunedin Star* – nearby which a crouching skeleton was found buried in the sand, and the *Eduard Bohlen* (*page 190*) – a 310 foot long, 2 272 gross tonne cargo ship that ran aground in 1909. With the slowly shifting, receding shoreline, the *Eduard Bohlen* curiously lies in its sandy grave almost half a kilometre from the water's edge.

Left: 'The Namib Kiss'

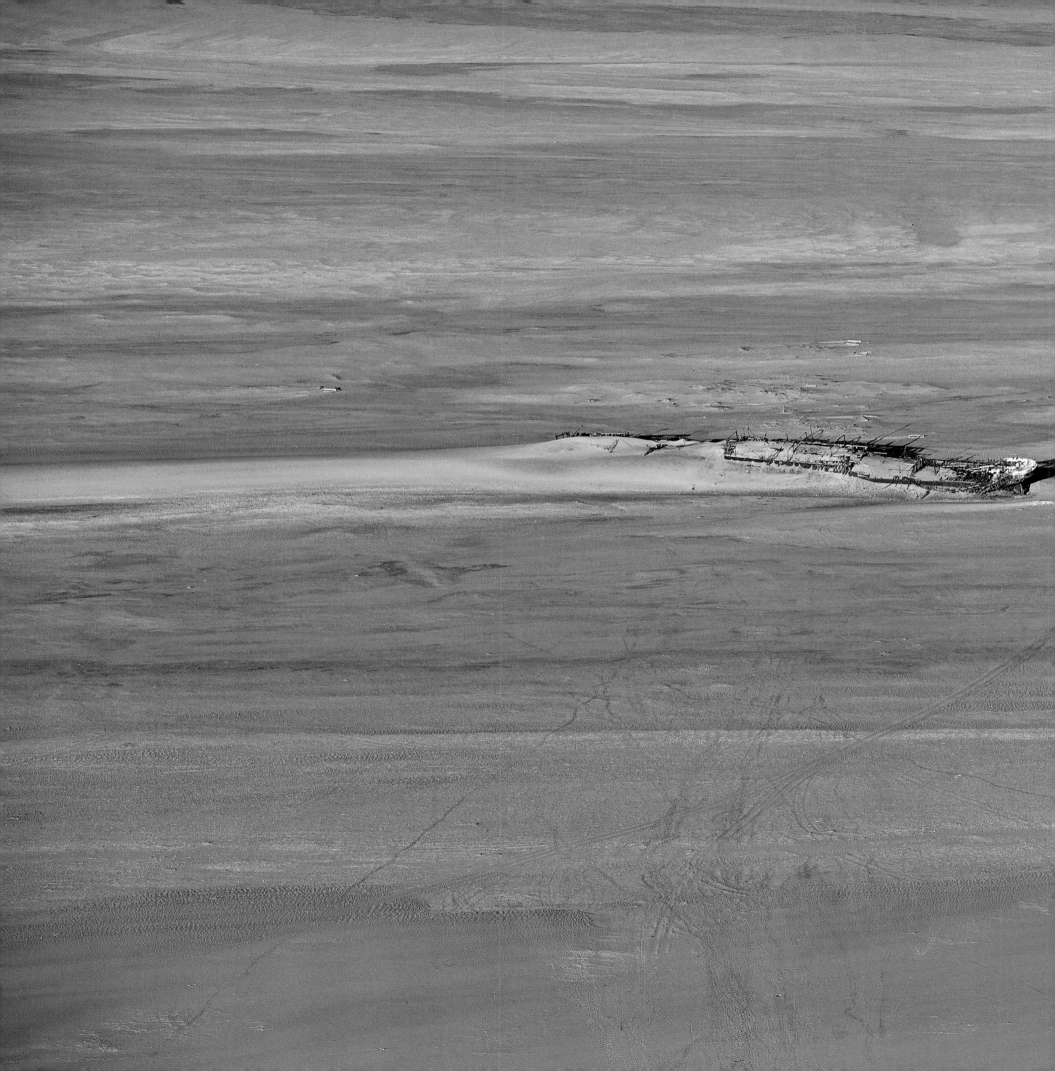

Camp Kipwe

TWYFELFONTEIN

Situated in the wild and rugged landscape of Damaraland, now known as the Kunene Region – one of Namibia's least populated areas, bounded by Ovamboland in the north and Windhoek in the south – is the charming and picturesque Camp Kipwe.

Ingeniously designed around the smooth granite boulders of the area, the exclusive luxury suite and nine innovative thatch-roofed igloo-shaped bungalows at Camp Kipwe are constructed of temperature-cooling stone. Incorporated boulders, small red basalt rocks and mopane branches help to blend the structures seamlessly into the surrounding rocky landscape, adding to its natural organic feel. Each of the bungalows are individually designed to make the most creative use of the adjacent boulders (including en-suite bathrooms, partially open to the starry African night sky) and the large shaded verandahs provide commanding panoramic views over the craggy kopjes, valleys and hills. Adding authenticity to the fun rustic theme, hot water is supplied by old-fashioned wood-burning 'donkey' boilers.

Kipwe (which means 'blessed' in Swahili) is one of several renowned properties created by the Visions of Africa group, each equally ground-breaking: Camp Kipwe's sister property, Mowani Mountain Camp (*page 196*) is mere moments away, and several properties that fall within the Onguma Game Reserve on the eastern side of Etosha complete the group's visionary trio.

The camp is well placed for exploring the attractions of Damaraland, which include nature drives in search of Namibia's elusive desert elephant, a creature surrounded by much romance and mystery. The desert-adapted elephants, which are slightly smaller than the African elephant, generally inhabit the ancient, ephemeral riverbeds that can be found in north-west regions of Namibia. The seasonal rivers are dependent on local rainfall before flowing above ground, however, in times of drought the water still flows, but deep under the desert sand. Great distances are covered in search of feeding grounds and scattered waterholes, sometimes up to 70 kilometres, as these remarkable desert giants intuitively follow centuries-old routes or 'elephant highways'.

Mowani
Mountain Camp

TWYFELFONTEIN

Set within a magic granite enclave, moments from sister property Camp Kipwe, is distinctive Mowani Mountain Camp. Perched high on a rocky outcrop, its thatch-roofed beehive domes are reminiscent of an African kingdom of old. Overlooking vast gravel plains to the mountains beyond, the mountain camp, with its three luxury suites and 12 rooms complete with truly breathtaking views, provides an ideal base to explore the unspoilt wilderness of southern Damaraland (now known as the Kunene Region), an area boasting magnificent desert scenery, mesmerising geological formations, remarkable archaeological sites and a unique variety of desert fauna and flora.

Although a place of deep tranquility, a plethora of activities are on offer – from lofty hot-air balloon trips over the Aba-Huab Valley and alfresco Champagne breakfasts beneath mopani trees to day-time game drives where local tribesmen assist in tracking the area's wildlife, including leopard, mountain zebra, kudu, springbok and klipspringer.

Mowani Mountain Camp is less than an hour away from Twyfelfontein – the site of one of the most spectacular, largest and longest-running outdoor art exhibitions in the world. Twyfelfontein is a rare example of ancient San engravings (more than 2 500!) and paintings occurring at the same site. The area has been inhabited for over 6 000 years, first by hunter-gatherers and later by Khoikhoi herders, both using it as a place of worship and a location to conduct shamanist rituals. In 2007 Twyfelfontein was designated the country's first World Heritage Site. The area was known as Ui-Ais, meaning 'jumping fountain', a name given to the spring by the Bergdama who once lived there. In recent times, the waters slowed to a hop and trickle and the area was renamed Twyfelfontein, meaning 'doubtful fountain'. The small spring has brought life to this thirstland for thousands of years. Stone Age people were probably attracted to the area by the presence of water and game, and their rock art depicts the richness of the wildlife once found there.

HIMBA

Kaokoland's statuesque, intricately-adorned residents of red ochre

Namibia's Himba people, statuesque and slender, with their distinctive customary fashion, plaited hairstyles and red ochre-adorned skin, are visually arresting and perhaps the best known of Namibia's tribes. Living throughout the Kaokoveld region (now known as the Kunene Region) in scattered settlements, their isolated existence has largely sheltered them from Western influence, safeguarding their traditional way of life that is lived today as it has been since their earliest days.

During the eighteenth century, the Herero migrated to central Namibia, and a group amongst them decided to remain in the Kaokoveld, subsequently developing their own traditions, yet maintaining their mother-tongue which they still share with the Herero people today. In the mid-1800s the separated tribe faced much hardship, becoming impoverished by Nama cattle raiders and forcing them to become hunter-gatherers. Because of these events they were called the 'Tjimba', derived form the word meaning aardvark – an animal that digs for its food. Many fled to Angola where they were called Ovahimba, meaning 'those who ask for help', and after the First World War they resettled in Kaokoland, eventually becoming one of the wealthiest cattle-herder nations in Africa.

The Himba remain semi-nomadic, moving constantly in search of grazing grounds and water for their cattle and goats, and are the most exclusively pastoral of all Bantu-language speakers in the country. The Himba have a richly layered tradition. Their tribal structure is based on bilateral descent – an advantageous system for groups that live in extreme environments, allowing individuals to rely on two sets of families dispersed over a wide area. Each tribe member belongs to two clans: a patriclan (through the father), called oruzo, and a matriclan (through the mother), called eanda. Himba clans are led by the eldest male. Sons live with their father's clan, and when daughters marry, they go to live with their husbands' clan.

In most villages women tend to perform the more labour-intensive work, such as carrying water to the village, milking the cows and building homes, while men are responsible for handling the political tasks and legal trials. Members of an extended family typically dwell in a homestead – a small, circular hamlet of huts and work shelters that surrounds an okuruwo (ancestral fire) and a central livestock enclosure or kraal. Both the fire and livestock are closely tied to their belief in ancestor worship, the fire representing ancestral protection and the livestock allowing 'proper relations' between human and ancestor. A monotheistic people, Himba worship the god Mukuru as well as the clan's ancestors, whom they believe act as representatives for Mukuru. Both are communicated with each week, when the designated 'fire-keeper' solemnly approaches the ancestral fire.

Like their Herero counterparts, the Himba have an extraordinarily innate sense of style, although their diversion in traditional dress couldn't be more different. While the Herero traditionally drape themselves from head-to-toe in flowing ohorokweva dresses, Himba women and men wear very little apart from skirts or loincloths made of animal skins in various colours. However, the Himba are lavish in their intricate hairstyles and customary adornments. Undoubtedly the most distinctive feature of the Himba tribe is the female tradition of applying a mixture of ground red ochre, animal fat and herbs to their faces and bodies. This age-old concoction, known as otjize, performs a number of functions aside from being consistent with the Himba ideal of beauty – it deeply nourishes and protects the skin from the harshness of the sun, acts as a natural insect repellent, and spiritually the red colour tinge that it gives the body is symbolic of earth's rich red colour and the blood that symbolizes life. Himba women use a separate mixture of butterfat, herbs and charcoal to rub on their hair, and 'steam' their clothes over the permanent fire, spending as much as three hours a day to wash and dress.

The diverse hairstyles of the Himba indicate age and social status. Young Himba boys typically wear a single ondato plait that falls down the back of the head. Once grown up and of marriageable age, men fashion two plaits, known as ozondato, and after marrying, the ombwiya headdress – a scarf made from fabric covering the hair and decorated with an ornamental band – is traditionally worn, as well as a number of plaits covered in the otjize mixture. Like the boys, young girls also wear their hair plaited, but from the time of puberty the girls' plaits are moved to the face over their eyes and they typically wear an ekori headdress made from tanned goat or sheepskin with three leaf-shaped points, usually decorated with iron beads.

The traditional Himba leather 'skirt' consists of two parts, with a larger skin (oruheke) at the back and a smaller one at the front. Although in earlier times calf leather was preferred, today these garments are also created out of ordinary cloth bought in shops. The waistband, consisting of several sections of iron beads, indicates that a woman has had more than one child. The thick shell-beaded necklaces worn by women are the equivalent of the ombongora necklaces worn by men. These signify that a woman is married and has children.

Cattle play a central and significant role in the lives of the Himba. Cows are often known by name, and their proud owners will regularly boast about the pedigree and milk-producing abilities of their herds. Sour milk (omaere) is a staple food, and small livestock, such as goats and sheep, are the main source of fresh meat. Animals follow the herdsmen and are taught to respond to their signals. Himba usually have favourite cows to which they pay special attention, a close relationship that is continued after death – a herdsman may be buried in the skin of a beloved animal and the horns of animals slaughtered for the funeral are sometimes used to adorn the grave.

The Otjikandero Himba Orphan Village, where these images were captured, is a special community in the heart of north-western Namibia, about 20 kilometres outside of Kamanjab. In 1999, local farmer Jaco Burger moved to Kaokoland to work and live with the local Himba tribe. There he met Uakurisa Mukajo Mbahono, the last queen in her bloodline of the Ovahimba tribe 'Mbahono', which came to Namibia during the Angolan war. Mukajo had suffered through leukemia and was unable to have children of her own – a fate, according to Himba custom, that precluded her from marrying a man from her tribe. Together Jaco and Mukajo looked after the village's orphans and soon became traditionally married. Jaco quickly became a respected part of the Himba village (and considered a chief in the Kamanjab and Kaokoland area), adopting their dress, lifestyle and speaking the Ovahimba language fluently. In 2001 the couple decided to move permanently with the orphaned Ovahimba children to Jaco's family farm in Kamanjab, where Otjikandero ('place of plenty milk') Himba Village Project was established. Today the lively traditional village is filled with the sounds of laughter, dancing, singing and animated Ovahimba chatter, as Himba adults and 36 orphaned children live a harmonious traditional Himba life.

The village's orphans come from difficult circumstances in Kaokoland, many having lost their parents to illness or accident. The project's main focus is to give the orphaned children a chance to grow up in their traditional fashion, lifestyle and culture. In order to sustain the project, related Himba families of the children were needed in close proximity in order to teach them their traditional ways. These Himba 'volunteers' stay between six and twelve months, together with their own children, in one of the four permanent Himba villages on the family farm before returning to Kaokoland.

Onjowewe 'Film' House

KAMANJAB

Deep in the region of Damaraland, now called the Kunene Region, and within walking distance from Otjikandero Himba Orphan Village is one of Namibia's special secret locations, Onjowewe House – a most unusual 'lodge', popular amongst locals and travellers in the know.

The surreal Robinson Crusoe-style house was constructed for a film set in 2004 on the Burger family's cattle farm. *Le piste* (also known as 'The Trail') was co-written and directed by Eric Valli, following his highly successful film *Himalaya,* which was Oscar-nominated for Best Foreign Film in 2000. The movie's plot focuses around Grace, a 14-year-old girl from Europe who, with the help of a knowledgeable Himba tribesman, searches for her father, a geologist kidnapped by diamond poachers. Their trail leads them on an adventure through the country and the diverse filming locations include Epupa Falls, the Skeleton Coast, Lüderitz, Walvis Bay and Kamanjab.

After filming was complete the Burger family decided to keep the inspired house and added some finishing touches whilst maintaining all of its delightful charm. A unique overnight experience for travellers, the multi-storey surreal wooden structure, nestled amidst colossal boulders, has been adapted into a charmingly quirky dwelling. With no electricity, night-time lighting is provided by kerosene lamps, bamboo torches, candles and stars – all part of the romantic ambience.

ETOSHA NATIONAL PARK

Africa's renowned 'great white place of dry water'

North-western Namibia's Etosha National Park is one of the world's most famous national parks. Amongst the largest in Africa, it stretches over a vast area of some 22 912 square kilometres of saline desert, savannah and woodlands, and most characteristically the Etosha Pan, a shallow depression of approximately 5 000 square kilometres which forms the heart of the park and gives it its defining mirage-horizoned imagery.

Etosha's pan was once part of an enormous inland lake fed by rivers from the north and east, before it dried up over 120 million years ago due to continental drift that changed the slope of the land and the course of the tributaries.

The park, which stretched from the Kunene and Hoarusib river mouths on the Skeleton Coast in the west to Namutoni in the east, was proclaimed a game reserve on 22 March 1907 by Dr Friedrich von Lindequist, the Governor of German South West Africa at the time. It was designated as *Wildschutzgebiet Nr. 2* (Game Reserve Number 2), in numerical order following *Wildschutzgebiet Nr. 1* (West Caprivi). Subsequent additions widened the park's borders to an immense area of approximately 80 000 square kilometres, making it the largest game reserve on the planet, but due to political considerations it was gradually decreased by 77 per cent to its current size. In 1967 the area was elevated to the status of National Park and renamed Etosha. The name Etosha (sometimes spelt Etotha in early literature) comes from an Oshindonga word meaning 'great white place' and refers to the Etosha Pan. The Hai//om called the pan *Khubus,* which means 'the totally bare, white place with lots of dust'.

Etosha's vegetation varies from dwarf shrub savannah and grasslands, which occur around the pan, to thorn-bush and woodland savannah throughout the park. The mopane tree, with its distinctive butterfly-shaped (bifoliolate) leaf and thin seed pod, is the most common of Etosha's trees, estimated to make up around 80 per cent of all trees in the park. The north-eastern corner of Etosha is dominated by *Acacia* and *Terminalia* trees and the area south of the sandveld is characterised by deciduous tamboti trees, renowned for their 'jumping beans'. Tamboti tree seeds become infested with the larvae of a small grey moth, which causes the seed to jump centimetres into the air! West of Okaukuejo is the well-known 'Sprokieswoud', also known as the 'Phantom Forest', which is the only location where the African moringa tree grows in a flat area.

Set amongst Etosha's distinctive backdrop is a great abundance of wildlife. One hundred and fourteen mammal species are found in the park, from large animals such as elephant, giraffe, blue wildebeest, mountain and plains zebra and hyaena, as well as the trio of big cats – lion, leopard and cheetah – to smaller but no less fascinating mammals such as jackal, bat-eared fox, honey badger, warthog and the diminutive Damara dik-dik. Several endangered species found within the park include the black-faced impala, which is endemic to north-western Namibia and south-western Angola, as well as the black rhino, whose numbers in Etosha represent one of the largest increasing populations of black rhino in the world, and following a genetic study in 2009 on the area's giraffes, scientists believe that the northern Namib Desert and Etosha National Park populations form a separate subspecies.

Etosha's summers are ideal for birdwatching. While game viewing benefits from dry conditions, the summer rains turn some of the park's vast pans into seasonal lakes, attracting migratory and wetland birds. Etosha is home to 340 bird species, about a third of which are migratory, including the European bee-eater and several species of wader. Birds range from sizeable record-breaking species such as ostrich (world's largest bird), kori bustard (world's heaviest flying bird) and martial eagle (Africa's largest eagle) to extraordinary colonies of greater and lesser flamingo, tens of thousands of which congregate in a flamboyance on the pan to breed during a good rainy season.

The park has three well-established rest camps: Okaukuejo, Namutoni and Halali, as well as the exclusive tourist resorts at Onkoshi and Dolomite Camp. The popular resort of Okaukuejo is famed for its floodlit waterhole, where visitors can view nocturnal wildlife activity from a viewing deck. Namutoni is characterised by its historic fort (rebuilt in 1957) around which it is centred, and Halali, the last-built (in 1967) of Etosha's original camps, is situated halfway between Namutoni and Okaukuejo. Offering dramatic vistas over the Etosha Pan, Onkoshi is an exclusive camp with just 15 chalets, ensuring a private, personal experience, and the picturesque Dolomite Camp is situated amongst the dolomite outcrops of the pristine western Etosha National Park.

The dolomite hills on the southern border of the park are known as *Ondundozonananandana*, a lengthy name roughly translating as 'a place where a young boy herding cattle went to never return' – most likely in reference to a high density of predators in the area. Perhaps less imaginative but still telling is the English name of Leopard Hills.

Etosha Mountain Lodge

GAME HUNTING SAFARIS

Bordering the south-western boundary of the Etosha National Park for a distance of 75 kilometres, Etosha Heights Game Safaris spans a vast 62 000 hectares of mopani tree-strewn savannah, open grassland and mountainous areas, encompassing over 35 species of game, making it the largest private hunting reserve in the country. Nestled amongst dolomite hills overlooking the magnificent mopani forest is Etosha Heights' luxurious Etosha Mountain Lodge – an exclusive intimate lodge with six lavish chalets and an indulgent Ovahimba Villa private suite, encircled in a 5 000-hectare hunt-free photographic zone.

Trophy hunting is a popular activity in Namibia, forming an ingrained part of Namibian culture and history, and attracting thousands of international hunters each year. Having evolved into a highly specialised industry, trophy hunting and conservation continuously work hand-in-hand and a strong emphasis is placed on sustainable use and proactive management – the basis for successful wildlife populations and biodiversity – while the significant income generated contributes strongly to Namibia's GDP and supports poverty alleviation in the country.

Hunting at Etosha Mountain Lodge is renowned the world over as one of the finest true African hunting safari experiences. Trophy hunting season stretches from February to the end of November, during which time guests can hunt a wide variety of game, in the company of a registered hunting guide, from lion, leopard and the black-faced impala (all strictly on quota and subject to special permits) to eland, blue wildebeest, Burchell's zebra, giraffe, greater kudu, hartebeest, oryx, springbok, steenbok, waterbuck, warthog, spotted hyaena, cheetah and jackal.

The tradition of bow-and-arrow hunting has been practised since the earliest record of human activity in Namibia and is famously associated with the ancient San tribes who would hunt with poisoned arrows. This pared-down method of hunting has recently resurfaced as a popular activity in an updated modern form, with bow-hunting for trophies legalised in Namibia in 1997. Adventurous Etosha Mountain Lodge guests, wanting to experience this prehistoric 'art' with a modern twist (using a long bow, recurve bow or compound bow) can hunt a wide range of wildlife, including small game such as rabbits, porcupine, African wildcat, springbok and Damara dik-dik; medium-sized game such as warthog, nyala, spotted hyaena and cheetah; and large game including oryx, kudu and waterbuck.

Etosha's elephants belong to the group of elephants in north-western Namibia and southern Angola. They are the tallest elephants in Africa, but mineral deficiencies mean that they have very short tusks. During the blazing heat of the day, elephants regularly enjoy wading, wallowing and splashing in mud baths to cool their sun-dried skin and provide relief from biting insects.

Although Etosha is famed for the Big Five, the park is also home to thousands of birds, including the majestic martial eagle (*top left*). Equally fascinating are the smaller creatures such as the adorable albeit frightfully shy lesser bushbaby (*top right*), the alert scrub hare (*bottom right*) and the ubiquitous ground squirrel (*bottom left*).

Dolomite Camp

WESTERN ETOSHA

Until recently, the expansive ecologically significant western section of Etosha – an area approximately one-third in size of the entire park – was off limits to mainstream tourism. In 2011, with the launch of Namibia Wildlife Resorts' fifth Etosha establishment, the pristine area of western Etosha was finally made accessible via the creation of Dolomite Camp.

Nestled in the dolomite outcrops with exclusive views over the western Etosha hills, salt pans and plains, Dolomite Camp is the first camp to be built on this side of Etosha, and being significantly smaller than the three more established camps of Okaukuejo, Halali and Namutoni, the emphasis is on a more luxurious, exclusive and intimate experience.

Designed by celebrated local interior designer Heidrun Diekmann, renowned for her archi-nature style, the 20 thatch-roofed, canvas-walled chalets are built on elevated wooden decks on and around the outer edges of the dolomite ridge, with breathtaking panoramic views from each. The camp's sumptuous interiors reflect some of the features of this part of the park, characterised by dolomite rock formations, mopane, moringa and savannah woodland.

The romantic dolomite hill setting of the camp is surrounded by an abundance of seasonally blooming plant species and an equally abundant array of wildlife. Here, amongst the surrounding *karstveldt* and mopane shrubland vegetation, which is unique to this section of Etosha, one can expect to see large herds of zebra, giraffe and antelope as well as elephant, leopard, lion and a prolific profusion of birdlife. The wildlife has developed in this special section of Etosha without human disturbance and rare species such as black rhino and black-faced impala have established themselves in healthy numbers and are regularly spotted amongst the 15 waterholes in the vicinity of the camp. Another special attraction exclusive to the area is the opportunity to see both the plains zebra and the mountain zebra in the same plains – a rare sight in the country.

Located on the western edge of the pan, 17 kilometres from the southern entrance of the park, Okaukuejo is the oldest tourist camp in Etosha and it currently functions as the administrative hub of the park, as well as being home to the Etosha Ecological Institute. Okaukuejo is famed for overlooking a large permanent waterhole which is floodlit at night. Here a wide diversity of wildlife

congregates and interacts – starting at the break of dawn, when animals such as springbok, elephant, lion and black rhino arrive in large numbers to quench their thirst, with the activity continuing throughout the day and deep into the night, particularly during the lengthy dry season.

Onkoshi Camp

ETOSHA

Namibia Wildlife Resorts' Onkoshi Camp, opened in late 2008, is the first new camp to be built inside the Etosha National Park in over 30 years. Arriving at Namutoni, guests are transported some 25 kilometres in safari vehicles to Onkoshi Camp in an exclusive north-eastern sandveld area of the park entirely out of view of current tourist routes.

Arrival at Onkoshi Camp immediately elicits a gasp of surprise – the luxurious stilted camp is nestled on the rim of a secluded peninsula saline pan, its immensity the very stuff of the African dream! The sprawling, flat pan has a life of its own – hot days bring shimmering mirages and with sunrise and sunset hues and moods change with each passing minute. The sense of silence, space and boundless freedom is tangible here.

With just 15 chalets – each elevated on wooden decks, with thatched roofs, canvas walls and large, wooden-framed retractable doors allowing spectacular panoramic views – the Onkoshi experience is as exclusively intimate as one can find in the national park.

In line with Namibia Wildlife Resorts' environmental policy, and following the lead of new safari lodges throughout southern Africa, Onkoshi was developed with low-impact construction and is maintained with renewable energy sources – each unit is energy self-sufficient, entirely from solar energy, including the water heating, lighting and power points.

Activities on offer at Onkoshi Camp include professionally guided game drives to the surrounding areas of the park (as well as exclusive access to otherwise-restricted areas), as well as remarkable moonlight walks on the Etosha Pan.

Onguma

THE FORT AND TENTED CAMP

Covering over 34 000 hectares of savannah, bushveld, omuramba and dry pan, and once part of greater Etosha, Onguma Game Reserve is undoubtedly one of Nambia's best-kept secrets. Situated on the eastern side of Etosha, bordering Fisher's Pan, the lush reserve is home to over 30 different animal species, including kudu, giraffe, eland, oryx, hartebeest, zebra and impala, as well as lion, leopard, cheetah and a family of rare black rhino. With over 300 bird species as well as the biggest breeding colony of white-backed vultures in Namibia, Onguma is also a birdwatcher's utopia – identified as one of the key birdwatching sites in southern Africa, particularly during the summer months when thousands of species migrate en-masse to wetlands created by the seasonal rains and ephemeral river systems.

In the local Herero language Onguma means 'the place you don't want to leave' and its various lodges, conceptualised by renowned local visionary André Louw (*page 225 right*) are amongst the finest in the country. Louw's Visions of Africa is also responsible for Camp Kipwe and Mowani Mountain Camp in Damaraland (now the Kunene Region) and the attention to detail, consideration of environment (both in responsibility and design) and charming eccentricity is equally evident amongst all their properties.

Onguma The Fort with its massive raw walls and picturesque stone-clad features is a striking combination of authentic Namibian and exotic Moroccan elements, giving it a unique atmosphere of fairytale-like adventure. Dramatic, iconic and sumptuously luxurious, The Fort overlooks the beautiful starkness of the Etosha Pans, dotted with hundreds of camelthorn trees and an abundance of wildlife. The sunset views, many claim, are the finest in the country when observed from the lodge's commanding tower, which overlooks the expansive sun-drenched landscape from its lofty height. Moments away the intimate **Onguma Tented Camp** provides a beguiling combination of luxury and African adventure with a 14-bed tented camp, built around an active waterhole that hums with day-long activity. Each of the seven spacious tents, with their peerless bush-chic styling and creature comforts to suit the most discerning of travellers, extends along a U-shaped design, allowing for maximum privacy and uninterrupted views of equally lush surrounds.

Mokuti Etosha Lodge

Hidden in between over 4 000 hectares of wildlife-filled farmland, Mokuti Lodge is a mere four minutes' drive from the eastern Namutoni Von Lindequist entrance gate, making it the closest lodge to Etosha National Park.

Mokuti in the local Ovambo language means 'in the forest' and upon entering one immediately encounters a lush oasis of luxury, nestled in and around verdant indigenous gardens, with bontebok grazing peacefully along the winding pathways between the traditional thatch-roofed chalets.

Mokuti's popularity, especially as an events and conference getaway, is not only due to its special location, but also the unusual number of facilities and activities on offer to suit every whim. For leisure there are two swimming pools, a children's splash pool, floodlit tennis courts and a state-of-the-art gym. Mokuti's indulgent, exclusive luxury spa is designed to fit within its unique natural surroundings of African bush terrain, characteristic mopane trees, rare birds and every so often a passing giraffe making its way to the waterhole adjacent to the spa's two outdoor relaxation areas.

Explorers can discover the fauna and flora of the area via walking trails, guided game drives to nearby Etosha or a brave visit to the lodge's own exclusive reptile park. Ontouka Reptile Park is the first and largest of its kind in Namibia. The educational park allows guests to see the country's elusive reptiles such as crocodiles, turtles, goannas and chameleons, although it is the vast array of snake species that the park is most well known for: from beautiful non-poisonous snakes that are found throughout Etosha, such as mole snakes, skaapstekers and egg eaters, to some of the world's most venomous and feared species, including puff adder, boomslang, black mamba, the western barred spitting cobra and the African coral snake.

Traditional local cuisine is served in an authentically African boma centred around a sizzling fire and enclosed with reeds and an African night sky. A popular explanation for the word 'boma' is that during British colonial times in Africa its letters stood for 'British Officers Mess Area'. While many defend this opinion, the Oxford English Dictionary ascribes the meaning to the considerably earlier use by the adventurer Henry Morton Stanley, in his book *Through the Dark Continent* (1878), perhaps borrowing the Swahili word for 'defended area' – *iboma*.

Frans Indongo Lodge

The magnificent Frans Indongo Lodge, a jewel in the Namibian thornbush savannah, is situated less than 50 kilometres from Otjiwarongo, in the proximity of the Waterberg Plateau Park. A popular stopover between Etosha and Windhoek, the lodge is placed within a sizeable 17 000-hectare game farm boasting an abundance of wildlife, including zebra, giraffe, gemsbok and lechwe as well as white and black rhino, black wildebeest and hartebeest. The lodge, as part of its active commitment to nature conservation, supports the Cheetah Conservation Fund as part of their popular excursions and Dr Frans Indongo is part of the custodianship programme for the endangered black rhino.

The lodge's distinctive character, with its elements of natural stone, wood and reed; earthen pots and carved wooden figure *objets d'art*; and surrounding tree-trunk fencing reminiscent of a *kraal* (traditional cattle enclosure), is unmistakably inspired by the traditional Ovambo style, a homage to the heritage of the celebrated owner, after which the lodge is named.

Frans 'Aupa' Indongo is one of Namibia's much-loved living legends, famed for his self-made business empire which today extends to almost all major sectors in the country, including fishing, farming, property, vehicle sales, fuel, manufacturing and hospitality. The famously hard-working Ovambo tycoon came from humble beginnings, tending his father's cattle from age seven while growing up in the northern Namibian village of Omusimboti where his family lived a peaceful life of subsistence farming. Indongo attended a nearby Finnish missionary school, although not without obstacles – during the rainy months cattle had to be kept from the mahangu fields, and Frans and his siblings would take turns going to classes. Nevertheless Frans excelled, particularly with his favourite subject – arithmetic. Amazed by the shops of Walvis Bay, a concept he had not come across in his home town, Indongo vowed to one day possess his own and with ammased savings of three pounds (sixty shillings) from brick laying for a local businessman he purchased a simple sewing machine to start a tailoring business.

Through perseverance and passion Indongo built a successful shopping complex in 1967, subsequently developing a business empire that today employs more than 1 400 people and has a gross investment in the country in excess of N$150 million. During the difficult times of apartheid, business for a young Ovambo man was continually challenging – special passes were needed to travel to Otjiwarongo (where he could buy commodities), it wasn't possible to stay in Windhoek hotels, and bank credit was unobtainable. A remnant from those difficult years is Frans Indongo's habit of concluding many of his business deals with cash – a trait that has brought him fame across the country.

Roy's Rest Camp

GATEWAY TO THE KAVANGO AND BUSHMANLAND

The one-of-a-kind Roy's Rest Camp is situated some 55 kilometres north of Grootfontein, perfectly positioned as a stopover point between Windhoek, central Namibia, Rundu and the Caprivi Strip. It forms a small part of the vast 2 800-hectare Elandslaagte farm – a farm once belonging to the Dorslandtrekker Alberts family and one of the oldest properties in the area, dating back to the early 1930s.

The inimitable charm of Roy's is unmistakable as one enters the private road, just off the Tsumkwe turn-off. A rustic larger-than-life African mobile playfully dangles with animal skulls, horns and dried tree trunks – a mere introduction to the intriguing 'afro-junkyard' treasure trove that awaits inside. An extention of owner Wimpie Otto's creative mind and hand, every inch of the camp is filled with curiously juxtaposed inspired artifacts collected over the years. A Victorian-era bath spills a constant stream of water into the large pool, corroded farm implements of a bygone age are arranged haphazardly throughout the grounds and the central lapa is filled with chunky wooden furniture, skulls, bones, gnarled trunks, memorabilia, and chairs with kudu-horn armrests. Hand-crafted giraffe and elephant children's play apparatus give new meaning to 'jungle gym', a few old wagon parts and wheels from the original 1930s farm form part of the milieu and a truly 'wireless' outdoor internet café (African style!) adds to the effortless laid-back charm and quirkiness of the place.

Roy's Rest Camp is famed for being the 'gateway to Bushmanland' and offers life-changing day trips to an authentic San village, some 86 kilometres away. The 'living museum' is a traditional Ju/'hoansi-San village, located in Grashoek on the western edge of Bushmanland, an area characterised by endless, open bushveld which extends over the border into Botswana and is the Ju/'hoansi-San's age-old home. Tours to the nomad village were initiated by local tour guide Werner Pfeifer and teacher Ghau N!aici and since 1995 it has been independently managed by the Ju/'hoansi-San community members, giving visitors insight into their ancient traditions and culture, including guided bush walks, art and crafts, group singing and healing trance dancing, as well as a chance to hear the distinctive 'click' language of the San.

THE SAN

Namibia's ancient people

The San people are the earliest known inhabitants of Namibia and are generally regarded as the oldest culture in the world, their existence dating back over 100 000 years. Legendary for their unparalleled knowledge of the land, exceptional hunting skills, primeval rock-art and complex 'click' languages, the semi-nomadic hunter-gatherer people, part of the Khoisan group and related to the traditionally pastoral Khoikhoi, have since time immemorial adapted remarkably well to their arid and uncompromising environment.

The San's lifestyle began to change about 2 000 years ago when a pastoral revolution drove Nguni people into the San's traditional hunting grounds. These pastoralists introduced a new way of life: cattle rearing and crop cultivation. Centuries later, Portugal's search for a sea route to India paved the way for European colonisation of the subcontinent. The newcomers brought firearms, notions of individual land ownership and strong prejudices against southern Africa's 'first' people. Combined, these factors led to marginalisation, enslavement and killing of the San. Today there are approximately 35 000 San people in Namibia, the majority living on farms in the eastern parts of the country or in remote communal areas in the Otjozondjupa and Omusati regions.

Historically, the San of Namibia are made up of a number of distinct groups: the Naró from the region of Omaheke, the Kxoe (often referred to as 'Black River Bushmen') who live in the Caprivi and adjacent areas of the Kavango region, the Hai-//om, who traditionally roamed the areas now known as Tsumeb, Otavi, Outjo and the Etosha National Park, and the /Auni, a small remnant of the near-extinct Cape Bushmen, living along the lower Nossob River in eastern Namibia. The !Xu are the largest single group of San, and within this group are the //Kx'au-//'en, who reside in the Gobabis region, the Zû-/hoasi of north-eastern Namibia and the !Õ-!Xu, who live in the woodlands of northern Namibia (their name translates as 'Forest !Xu').

For most of their existence, the various San groups have had little or no contact with one another, resulting in varying traditions and different languages. To hear the unique 'click' languages of the San is a fascinating experience. There are five types of click sounds, although not all of them are used in any single dialect. Each click sound is created by a varied sucking action of the tongue and modern methods of 'spelling' these sounds include punctuation marks such as / (dental), ≠ (palatal), ! (alveolar or retroflex) and // (lateral).

In 2009, four textbooks for children were published with the support of ICEIDA (The Icelandic International Development Agency) in two San languages – Kwedam (spoken by approximately 5 000 San in Western Caprivi) and !Xun (spoken by a similar number of San in the Mangetti area of Otjozondjupa). This exciting project has helped to build the foundation for the San's future education, cultural awareness and pride, and record the intricacies of an endangered language for posterity.

Perhaps no other groups of people in the world's history are as masterful at both hunting and gathering as the San. Various methods of hunting are used, depending on the season, environment and game that is being hunted. Synonymous with San hunting is the bow and arrow, the San's most popular weapon. Bows are made from the flexible branches of the raisin bush, and their strings from thick sinews, while arrows are stored in a cylindrical quiver, made from the root-bark of an *Acacia* tree. A wide range of purpose-specific natural poisons are used, some derived from plants such as *Adenium boehmianum* and *Euphorbia subsala,* while others come from snakes (puff adder and cobra) and even the larvae of *Polyclada* and *Diamphidia* beetles.

Each day, San women stroll the veld in search of food. The !Xu know more than 80 species of edible plants, fruits, berries, nuts, bulbs and tubers, the most popular of which is the abundant and highly nutritional mangetti nut or, during springtime, succulent moisture-rich tsamma melons.

The wealth of rock paintings and engravings found in mountains and hills throughout Namibia, the oldest of which dates back some 28 000 years, bear witness to the San's former habitation in many parts of the country. Famous examples include the White Lady painting of the Brandberg and the rock engravings at Twyfelfontein, one of the richest collections in Africa. The San used different coloured stones – typically finely ground red rock mixed with animal fat – as a simple yet powerful concoction able to withstand harsh weather and long periods of time.

Left: San elder reaching a trance state with the aid of repetitive, rhythmic clapping

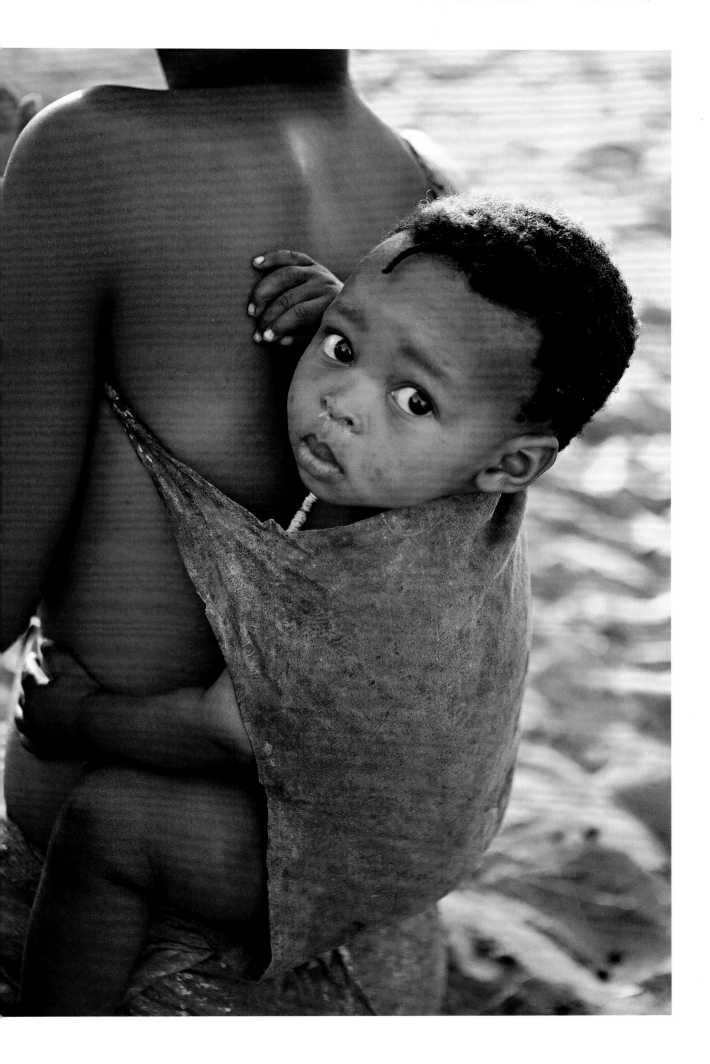

The traditional San way of life, while initially viewed as 'primitive' by early European settlers, is not only rich in knowledge and tradition but also remarkably attuned to individual and communal well-being. The naturally egalitarian society of the San was built on mutual respect amongst age and gender, and although many tribes had hereditary chiefs, their authority was limited. San women enjoy a status of great respect in the community, making important family decisions, gathering food and occasionally taking part in hunting as well. Children are given no social duties other than to spend their time playing. In fact, throughout all the ages of a San's life, great value is placed on leisure time.

San villages are, at many times, a place of song, dance and laughter. Any special occasion and excitement provokes singing and dancing and at any given time imaginative and ancient games are played amongst the whole village. Perhaps unique to the San culture, the entire village partake in games where no differentiation is made on account of age and both young and old play and laugh alike – a perfect illustration of the joyful San way of embracing life. Plays are common too, where all the members of the village act out their special part in the retelling of age-old legends with prose and skilful mimicry, to the rhythmic sounds of clapping, stomping and chanting. The rattle, a musical instrument commonly used by the San, is made of the fruit of the *Strychnos spinosa* plant. The inside of the fruit is eaten and then filled with seeds and sealed. To provide rhythm and sounds as they dance, moth cocoons filled with stones or seeds are attached around their ankles. A popular San instrument is the hunter's bow, strung with animal hair and equipped with a hollowed-out melon or empty tin can as a sound box.

As the popular San legend recalls, Pisiboro (a loutish trickster regularly featured in San stories) one day came across Ostrich (a half human/half animal hybrid from the 'People of the Early Race') eating berries in the bush. When Ostrich raised his arms to pick more berries, Pisiboro noticed the smell of burning and a clump of hot coals hidden beneath Ostrich's arms. These were times of total darkness and the only way the people knew how to make fire was to wait for after the rains when rainbows would appear and the red colour could be thrown onto the ground to ignite flames. So intrigued was Pisiboro by Ostrich's secret, that he returned again, this time snatching the hot coal from Ostrich's armpit and fleeing, eventually shattering it into small pieces. Then he told the fire to hide, and it concealed itself in the stones and in the branches of the brandybush, from which the San have made their fire sticks ever since. Pisiboro then made a *djani* weighted with a burning coal, but while playing with it, his clumsiness caused the fiery *djani* to fly so high that it remained in the sky and became the sun.

Although the San's tales regarding the origin of fire differ considerably from tribe to tribe, all share one common element– the *djani*. Also known as the *zani* by the /Gwi, this popular children's toy has amused San children for millennia – in fact, the San believe that its origins date back to a mythical time when animals were still humans. The *djani* is made from a 35-centimetre length of hollow reed, with small, soft guinea fowl under-feathers stuck into one end and a short thong, weighted with a nut, fastened to the other. A large symmetrical burnt-edged feather is bound to the reed shaft in a similar fashion, slightly above the mid-point and curving outward to give the toy its spin. The age-old 'spinning top' is kept in the air for as long as possible, as young children dash hither and thither beneath it, excitedly whipping it back into the air with long sticks. According to traditional San folklore, if it were not for the *djani*, the world would sill be covered in darkness.

Driving along the lengthy dusty route to Rundu, travellers experience a road-side view of the colourful day-to-day activities of Namibia's north. Locals regularly walk extensive distances to fetch water, go to school, attend a church service, or meet with friends, and always with warm and friendly faces. Cart rides are a welcome respite for easing the distances, particularly amongst the elderly. Many carts are home-

branded with well-known international marques such as Ford, John Deere or Massey Ferguson (sometimes curiously spelt 'Messey Frocoson'). Here road-side craft stalls are amongst the finest in the country: a wood-carved model aeroplane, complete with engine specifications on the wings and a telephone number for enquiries along the fuselage, is a typical example of the loving attention to detail found here.

Kaisosi
River Lodge

Set directly on the banks of the perennial Okavango River, encircled with the sounds of frogs, peacocks and exotic birds, is the popular Kaisosi River Lodge – a well-known stopover en route to the Caprivi and the Popa Falls.

Whether staying in one of the thatch-roofed chalets or camping or caravanning, the lodge, with its unique location, offers a wide variety of activities to explore the region, well known for its beautiful landscapes and radiant sunsets. Exploring the picturesque Okavango River, guests can start their morning with a tranquil floating breakfast, cruising gently along the banks of Namibia and Angola, and the lodge can accommodate groups of up to 30 guests on a breathtaking sunset river cruise. The area is home to a dazzling array of birds including Pel's fishing owl, slaty egret, carmine bee-eaters and the resplendent African fish eagle. As an example of the sheer biodiversity, over 40 different species of dragonfly exist in the surrounding area alone! Fishing for tilapia, catfish and tigerfish amongst this serene backdrop is another hugely popular activity.

The lodge is situated just seven kilometres from the north-eastern town of Rundu, the Kavango's capital, famed for its locally made crafts and wood carvings – the skills for which have been passed down through the generations.

Tours can be arranged to visit a nearby traditional Kavango village, the spirited local market in Rundu and the fascinating Mbunza Living Museum, giving visitors a glimpse into the life and traditions of the local people. If so inclined, shebeen-hopping in Rundu is an experience not-to-be-missed – characteristic of the northern regions, the town is dotted with small, trendy, informal bars known as 'Cuca shops'. Their name is derived from a Portuguese make of Cuca beer, popular in neighbouring Angola during the 1970s, and they typically serve the home-grown alcoholic tipple of choice, *ohikundu*, made from mahangu cereal. Cuca shops are renowned for their colourful names, such as 'The Dog is Hot', 'Put More Fire' and 'Joubek City'.

CAPRIVI

Namibia's lush far north-eastern Eden

In remarkable contrast to the country's characteristic landscapes of sandy dunes, vast panoramic vistas and rugged landscapes, the Caprivi (commonly known as the 'Caprivi Strip') is Namibia's easternmost region, as well as its wettest – a fertile wilderness of lush tropical vegetation, riverine forests and open woodland, all nourished by relatively high summer rainfalls and a complex network of perennial rivers and extensive flood plains.

The narrow strip of land, protruding from the north-east corner of Namibia, is around 450 kilometres long, approximately 100 kilometres wide, and is almost entirely surrounded by foreign countries. In the north-west it borders the Cuando Cubango Province of Angola, to the south is the North-West District of Botswana and in the north the Caprivi borders the Western Province of Zambia. Its short Okavango connection in the west and is its only domestic border. The Namibia-Zambia-Botswana tripoint lies less than 100 metres from the Zimbabwe border and, as such, Namibia is sometimes erroneously thought to border Zimbabwe.

The Caprivi is surrounded by four perennial rivers – Chobe, Kwando, Linyanti and the mighty Zambezi – and contains several National Parks – Bwabwata National Park, Mudumu National Park and Nkasa Rupala (formerly Mamili) National Park. With its lush vegetation and remote location, it is no surprise that the Caprivi is a wildlife paradise. The region is home to over 450 animal species, including lion, leopard, hyaena and cheetah, as well as a variety of water-adapted antelope such as puku and sitatunga. Herds of elephant are a regular sight in the Caprivi, with the area acting as a 'corridor' for African elephant moving from Botswana and Namibia into Angola, Zambia and Zimbabwe. Notably, the region provides significant habitat for the critically endangered African wild dog, and here you might catch a glimpse of Namibia's last surviving packs.

One of the area's main attractions is its prolific bird life, with around 70 per cent of Namibia's bird species (many of which are indigenous to the Caprivi area) being recorded here. The Caprivi's subtropical vegetation – filled with nearly 200 kinds of flora, shrubs, trees and fruits – is much like that of the Okavango's Kalahari woodland, but the Caprivi's trees generally grow taller because of the more favourable climate. Characteristic of the region are very tall mopane trees, dolfhout, wild lilac and Rhodesion teak, as well as the distinctive baobab.

Until the end of the nineteenth century the area was known as Itenge and was under the rule of the Lozi kings. During the late nineteenth century this strategic strip of land formed part of the British protectorate of Bechuanaland, now known as Botswana. In terms of the Zanzibar Treaty – concluded in July 1890 between Germany and Great Britain – Germany acquired the Caprivi Strip and the strategically important North Sea island of Heligoland in return for ceding its rights to the spice island of Zanzibar, and the African coast between the Witu and Juba rivers to Great Britain. The thin spur of land gave Germany access to the Zambezi River and provided a link with its colonial territory in East Africa. This new addition to German South West Africa was named after Count Georg Leo von Caprivi di Caprara di Montecuccoli, German chancellor from 1890 to 1894.

The capital of Caprivi was originally at Schuckmansburg until 1935, when it moved to Katima Mulilo, a name that means 'quenches the fire', referring to nearby rapids in the Zambezi. The town is situated on the bank of the Zambezi River and is surrounded by lush riverine vegetation that is home to abundant wildlife, including tropical birds and monkeys.

Today, approximately 80 000 people live in the Caprivi, making up about four per cent of Namibia's population. Most Caprivian communities are distributed along the riverbanks, major roads and in and around the lively town of Katima Mulilo, as well as within the region's villages – Sibinda, Sangwali, Linyanti, Chinchimane, Bukalo, Ngoma and Isize. Of Namibia's 13 regions, the Caprivi is the only one to boast six ethnic tribes – the Masubia, Yeyi, Mafwe, San, Tortela and Mbukushu – and due to the area's remoteness, most still live an unhindered traditional way of life. Most Caprivians make their living on the riverbanks. Freshwater fish are an important resource, providing food and income, as is stock farming (in particular of the long-horned indigenous Sanga breed of cattle, an animal steeped in social, religious, economic and mythical significance) and crop farming, primarily of the staple *mahangu* (pearl millet).

The ancient craft of basket weaving is widely practiced in northern Namibia. Wares are produced both for the local market as a source of income, as well as for use in local farming where baskets and trays are still used in the fields for carrying crops and winnowing grain. The leaves of the makalani palm are used to make the baskets, while colour is introduced through dyes extracted from local plant sources. The bark of the bird plum tree is commonly boiled with palm leaves to create a brown colour.

Flowing swiftly towards its delta deep in the Kalahari, the Kavango River rushes down a series of rapids known as Popa Falls. The name is deceptive though: the 'falls' are really a profusion of gentle rapids conveyed a mere four metres over rocky ledges in the riverbed. The Popa Falls are majestic, especially at daybreak, when the light filters through the surrounding foliage and illuminates

the fine mist rising from the cascading water. Situated in a protected national park area, the dense stands of trees that line the banks are ideal havens for birds such as osprey, Ayres's hawk eagle and orange-breasted bush-shrike. Despite the tranquility of the scene, swimming here is forbidden – within these deceiving waters lie hippos and crocodiles.

Nunda River Lodge

DIVUNDU

Set on the Okavango River, moments downstream from the popular Popa Falls, is the prominent Nunda River Lodge. The grand scale, thatch-roofed lapa complex of the lodge houses its many luxurious amenities and leads out onto a sizeable wooden deck, which overlooks the awe-inspiring scenery of the serene Okavango River. Acting as a watery border between Namibia and southern Angola, the Okavango is home to an estimated 430 species of birds, with over 20 endemic or near-endemic species, including the yellow wagtail, wattled crane, great snipe, African rail and African skimmers. Large herds of hippo snort and cavort in the surrounding waters, crocodiles bask on the banks and both locals and Angolans are regularly ferried between the neighbouring banks in *mokoros* (traditional dug-out canoes).

The lodge's accommodation, set amongst large shady trees and shrubs, consists of lavish thatched bungalows and luxury Meru tented chalets, each with their own deck overlooking the river, as well as camping sites moments from the riverbank. Amongst the many activities on offer, fishing for enticing species such as tilapia, sharptooth catfish, nembwe, as well as the legendary tigerfish is particularly popular. Open vehicles are also on standby to take guests on daily excursions to the close-by Mahango Game Reserve and Bwabwata National Park, where an abundance of wildlife can be experienced, such as the elusive wild dog, lion, leopard, buffalo, lechwe and sitatunga, as well as the largest herds of sable and roan antelope on the continent.

Cultural walks to local traditional villages can also be arranged. The immediate area is a homeland to two main tribes – the bantu-speaking Mbukushu, descendent from the great lakes of East Africa, and the Mbarakwengo, a San group, historically part of the larger Hukwe group, that are further split between clans in the far northern Kalahari and others that settled in south-eastern Angola. Sheltered by the sheer remoteness of the region, both tribes enjoy a peaceful existence, continuing to live their lives in an unhindered, age-old way.

The Caprivi, with its complex network of perennial rivers, riverine forests and fertile flood plains is an unusually flat area – here no piece of land is more than 47 metres higher than the rest. Scattered huts and sprawling rural populations are characteristic in the remote region, where innumerable small villages line the main roads and their inhabitants go about their lives in traditional custom.

Agriculture is the most important livelihood activity and there is a strong reliance on the use of natural resources such as wood for fuel and building, grass for thatching, veld foods (such as waterlily bulbs) and fish. Wealth is traditionally invested in cattle, which, besides having a strong social value, are also used to plough fields and draw carts – still a popular means of transport seen along the roads of the Caprivi.

Ngepi Camp

Situated in the unspoilt upper reaches of the Okavango Delta panhandle in the western Caprivi strip, the enchantingly secluded Ngepi Camp has earned a legendary status for its beguiling mix of strictly stress-free, fuss-free ambiance, harmonious surroundings-inspired accommodation, breathtaking riverside vistas and ever-present playful humour…not to mention their famous ablution facilities (more about that later).

Visionary owner, Mark Adcock, founded and designed the extraordinary camp as part of a soul-searching life journey, seeking a deeper meaning to existence beyond the inevitable rat-race routine of the corporate world, in which he had proved commercially successful. The faraway lush location on the pristine banks of the Okavango River is filled with the sounds of twittering birds (over 500 species are found here), cavorting hippos and crocodiles, and soul-nourishing serenity, and it is at this spot that Mark found his inner-peace and has ever since endeavoured to share it with all those who visit.

Ngepi's distinctive open-walled tree houses are each individually and organically designed and their east-facing position allows for a timely natural wake-up service with 'sunrise between your toes'. Ngepi's accommodation extends to magical bush huts and a bustling camping site along the tree-lined grassy riverbank that overlooks the Bwabwata National Park.

Although serenity is the order of the day, one sometimes needs a jam-packed day of activity to allow for reflection – and Ngepi's offerings are abundant. Its enviable position nestled between Mahango Game Reserve, mere kilometres to the south, and Bwabwata National Park directly opposite across the river, provides a wealth of wildlife – from elephant, lion and leopard to rare species such as wild dog and sable and roan antelope. Then there are guided bird and cultural village walks, catch-and-release fishing excursions, sunset cruises, volley ball, Frisbee golf, river rafting, authentic *mokoro* adventures and a chance to dip into Ngepi's unique 'floating swimming pool' in the river!

For most visitors the first excursion of discovery at Ngepi is visiting the myriad fun signs that pop up at every turn – each more hilarious and thought provoking than the next: 'Complaint box is in the river…beware of the crocodiles!', 'We love our grass and our kids, please don't park on either' and 'All prices subject to customer attitude' are some of many. Ngepi's ablution facilities are an attraction in themselves – from the open-air 'Adventure Outdoors Unlimited Star Bathroom' to the picturesque 'View with a Loo' and the rather opposingly-decorated 'His 'n Hers' – a guaranteed chuckle. As one learns to expect, there's a mindful Ngepi word of advice nearby: 'Caution: please sit down when toilets are in use'.

The Caprivi is home to several tribes, including the Mafwe and Masubia to the east of the Kwando River and the Mbukushu along the bank of the Kavango River. Adorned with hundreds of clattering bamboo beads, the traditional healer of Choi cultural village in the eastern Caprivi dances vigorously to the rhythmic clapping and chanting of local women. The Sikwekwe dancers of the Choi village are

renowned for their emotive and complex traditional dancing, and they have travelled the country to showcase their cultural rhythms, earning them fame as the finest dancing group in the region. Traditionally during these ceremonies, ancestral spirits are summoned with the aid of accoutrements, ritual objects and trance dancing. In addition, advice is given to the sick and troubled.

Susuwe Island Lodge

KWANDO RIVER

Susuwe Island Lodge is simply the stuff of dreams. Exclusive, private, remote and perfectly harmonised within its stunningly wild location overlooking the Kwando River, the lodge is renowned as an ideal spot for honeymooners and those simply in love with the romance of the African bush.

Susuwe Island is embedded in a lush, riverine forest, situated in the heart of the Bwabwata National Park, in north-east Namibia. The Susuwe concession, and the adjacent Kwando area, is one of the largest unfenced wilderness areas in southern Africa, and is filled with a wealth of flora and fauna-rich habitats, including riverine forests, savannahs, wetlands and Kalahari woodlands. Here wildlife viewing is spectacular with the river's permanent water source nourishing its delicate ecosystems and sustaining varied game and birdlife in the region. Over 8 000 elephant inhabit the area, and a trip to the nearby Horseshoe Bend, a unique oxbow lake that has formed on the Kwando River, is one of the region's famous attractions – here one can experience the overwhelming sight of the massive elephant herds that come each day to drink. Open 4x4 game drives in the park are never without action – the pristine setting is home to vast herds of roaming buffalo, lion, leopard, hippo, lechwe, sable and roan, as well as many rare and endemic bird species, including the wattled crane, racket-tailed roller, wood owl and African crake.

Developed as a joint venture with the Mayun Conservancy, which works with the local community and employs people in conservation initiatives (including an anti-poaching unit), Susuwe Island Lodge is itself an attraction of the area. The expansive main thatch-roofed lodge building is centred around a flickering fire pit – a popular evening spot where guests share stories of adventure under the starry canopy of the African sky. An extensive patio overlooks the picturesque vistas of the Kwando River and, rising high into the forest canopy of shady leadwood and mangosteen trees, a two-tiered bird viewing deck cradled in the arms of a giant African tree gives unique views over the magnificent savannahs, ancient Kalahari woodlands and sparkling wetlands below.

Lianshulu Lodge

MUDUMU NATIONAL PARK

Set on the banks of the magnificent meandering Kwando River, under a riverine forest canopy of shady jackalberry and mangosteen trees, lies the renowned Lianshulu Lodge, surrounded by a pristine wilderness of open savannahs, bushveld, wetlands and Kalahari woodlands.

The lodge, which was one of the first private luxury lodges to be built inside a Namibian national park, is located on an 800-hectare private concession inside the Mudumu National Park. With the Okavango River to the west and the mighty Zambezi to the east, and sharing a common border with neighbouring Botswana's legendary wildlife reserves, here one finds an extraordinary array of fauna and flora. Wildlife concentrations are at their highest during the winter season, where one can expect to see an abundance of elephant, buffalo, lion, leopard, zebra and giraffe. Summer conditions, however, transform the wilderness into a dazzling display of life and colour, and birdwatching is at its best.

The staff and management of Lianshulu Lodge proactively promote environmental education and wildlife conservation in its broadest sense, in order to create direct economic and social benefits to local communities. Actively encouraging projects that utilise indigenous products and knowledge on a sustainable basis, the lodge's extraordinary thatched public area, housing the plush dining, lounge and bar areas, has been constructed using local craftsmen and natural materials, to an awe-inspiring effect. The lodge was also instrumental in setting up the well-known Lizauli Traditional Village, which, while directly benefiting the local community, educates guests from around the world about traditional Caprivian lifestyles, providing insight into the local diet, fishing and farming methods, village politics, music and traditional medicine.

Lianshulu Lodge opens out onto spacious, split-level wooden decks, affording sweeping views over the Lianshulu Lagoon, a view also overlooked from each of the 11 generously-spaced chalets, all with their own private viewing decks, under the shade of the riparian forest canopy.

INDEX

Page numbers in **bold** indicate photographs.

SELECT BIBLIOGRAPHY

Diemont, M. 2012. *Beyond the Orange*. Cape Town: Historical Media

Dowson, T. and Lewis-Williams, D. 1989. *Images of power: understanding Bushman rock art*. Johannesburg: Southern Book Publishers

Estes, R.D. 1993. *The safari companion: A guide to watching African mammals*. Johannesburg: Russel Friedman Books

Goldbeck, M. 2012. *Gondwana History; Memorable Moments from Namibia's Past*. Third Edition. Windhoek: Nature Investments

Goldbeck, M., Greyling, T., Swilling, R. 2011. *Wild Horses in the Namib Desert*. Windhoek: Friends of the Wild Horses

Hockey, P., Dean, W. and Ryan, P. (eds). 2005. *Roberts birds of southern Africa*. Seventh edition. Cape Town: John Voelcker Bird Book Fund

Knappert, J. 1981. *Namibia: land and people, myths and fables*. Leiden: E.J. Brill

Lancaster, N. 1989. *The Namib sand sea: dune forms, processes and sediments*. Rotterdam: A.A. Balkema

Malan, J.J. 2012. *Peoples of Namibia*. Wingate Park: Rhino Publishers

Noli, G. 2010. *Desert Diamonds*. Plettenberg Bay: Hans Günther Noli

Schneider, G. 2008. *The Roadside Geology of Namibia 2*. Revised edition. Stuttgart: Gebrüder Borntraeger

Schoeman, A. 2010. *Skeleton Coast*. Windhoek: Venture Publications / Protea Book House

Siskonen, H. 1990. *Trade and socio-economic change in Ovamboland 1850–1901*. Helsinki: Historiallinen Seura

Van Schalkwyk, P. 2013. *Namibia Holiday & Travel*. Windhoek: Venture Publications

Wicht, H. 1969. *The indigenous plants of southern Africa*. Cape Town: Howard Timmins

SELECTED WEBSITES

abenteuerafrika.com
alter-action.info
bagatelle-kalahari-gameranch.com
brigadoonswakopmund.com
capecross.org
caprivicollection.com
cornerstoneguesthouse.com
desertbreezeswakopmund.com
deserthomestead-namibia.com
erindi.com
etoshahunting.com
etusis.de

gondwana-collection.com
guesthouse-swakopmund.com
heinitzburg.com
hoodiadesertlodge.com
indongolodge.com
joesbeerhouse.com
kaisosiriverlodge.com
kipwe.com
midgardcountryestate.com
mokutietoshalodge.com
mowani.com
namibfilms.com

namibiadesertexplorers.com
ngepicamp.com
norotshamaresort.com
nundaonline.com
nwr.com.na
okakambe.iway.na
meyerstours.com
omuntugarden.com
onguma.com
placeshilton.com/windhoek
rivercrossing.com.na
roidina-centaurus.com

roysrestcamp.com
sandfieldsguesthouse.com
sandwich-harbour.com
scenic-air.com
schroeder-estate.com.na
skydiveswakop.com.na
solitaireguestfarm.com
the-tug.com
thegourmet-restaurant.com
thestiltz.com
tommys.iway.na
weckevoigts.com